1993

Leadership in Middle Level Education

Volume I:
A National Survey of Middle Level Leaders and Schools

■ Jerry W. Valentine ■ Donald C. Clark ■
■ Judith L. Irvin ■ James W. Keefe ■
■ George Melton ■

About the Authors

Jerry Valentine is professor of educational administration, College of Education, University of Missouri, Columbia

Donald C. Clark is professor of secondary education, University of Arizona, Tucson

Judith L. Irvin is professor of middle education, Florida State University, Tallahassee

George Melton is deputy executive director emeritus, National Association of Secondary School Principals

James W. Keefe is director of research, National Association of Secondary School Principals

Contents

Advisory Committee

James Anding

James Aseltine

Don Dalton

Marion Payne

Lori Simmons

Joseph Tafoya

Sue Carol Thompson

Research Team for the Study

Jerry Valentine, Chairman

Donald C. Clark

Judith L. Irvin

James W. Keefe

George Melton

Tables

Tables

Foreword

The National Association of Secondary School Principals (NASSP) is committed to the study of middle level school leaders and programs on a systematic basis. This commitment extends to all levels of secondary education, including intermediate, middle, and junior high schools.

This publication is the first of two volumes in the National Study of Leadership in Middle Level Education. It reports survey data from a national sample of middle level principals on the personal and professional traits of principals, their job tasks and problems; on school programs; and on selected educational issues. Leadership profiles of principals and programs will be found in Chapter 5, along with notable findings and conclusions. This volume does not include all the information gathered from principals' responses to the survey questionnaires, but data tapes are available to researchers and other persons or organizations interested in the comprehensive file.

The NASSP is grateful to the Advisory Committee and the Research Team for their time and talent. Special thanks go to Jerry Valentine and Donald Clark for again providing creative scholarship on the national research team. The study could not have been completed, of course, without the generous cooperation of the principals and their schools.

Contemporary research stresses the importance of the principal to effective schooling and emphasizes the focal position of the principal as planner, leader, and facilitator. Research also documents the importance of other school leaders to the success of middle level schools. This study investigates leader and program characteristics that influence school operation and reports important trends and beliefs that most directly affect student success. It chronicles the story of middle level education today with its growing pains and its promise for the future.

James W. Keefe
NASSP Director of Research

Introduction

Middle level education is firmly anchored in the realities of human growth and development. Every practice advocated by middle level leaders and scholars is directly related to and compatible with the nature and needs of this special age level (Lounsbury, 1991, p. 68). The term "developmental responsiveness" (Lipsitz, 1984, p.6) is commonly used in middle level education to describe the effort to provide an educational setting that meets the unique needs of the pre and early adolescent. In 1981, NASSP's *National Study of Middle Level Principals and Programs* concluded that "middle level education was fast becoming a unique entity providing a discernible bridge between elementary and secondary education" (Valentine et al., 1981). Has the identity of the "middle level" continued to evolve? And more important, are evolving middle level schools developmentally responsive? Has current practice evolved and is practice congruent with the knowledge base of middle level education?

Periodically, NASSP studies current practice in order to inform educators and shape future practice. In 1966 and in 1981, NASSP sponsored national studies of middle level education. In fact, the terms "middle level education" and "middle level schools" were first used in the 1981 study (Clark and Clark, in press), and evidence was cited that the leaders and programs of "junior highs" and "middle schools" of the '70s were more alike than different. At that time, the middle level was in transition from childhood to adolescence, from mini-high school to unique program. The late '70s were the formative years, with expectations high, and behavioral and personality changes constant. In the '80s, the arguments about junior high versus middle school subsided as the concept of a "middle level" clearly emerged. Lounsbury (1991) has succinctly chronicled this evolution of middle level education in this century. Yet, as education moved into the '90s and headed toward the turn of the century, many current issues about middle level education and its leaders still needed attention. For example:

- Are there differences in the preparation and beliefs of middle level principals, assistant principals, and members of school leadership teams—the persons who will guide the schools into the next century?
- Is the leadership of today's middle level schools different from 1981 and 1966?
- Has the concept of a "leadership team" emerged in middle level schools?
- What are the beliefs of middle level educators about specific educational programs, and are the programs in middle level schools congruent with those beliefs?
- Are the programs in today's middle level schools different from those reported in previous studies?
- What practices are used in middle level schools experiencing successful restructuring of their programs?

To answer these and numerous other questions, the National Association of Secondary School Principals identified a research team and commissioned this comprehensive study of middle level education. The specific purposes of the study were the following:

1. Develop a contemporary base of knowledge about middle level principals, assistant principals, and leadership team members, including personal characteristics, job roles and tasks, and professional beliefs
2. Describe similarities and differences among these three groups of middle level leaders
3. Develop a base of knowledge about middle level programs and instructional practices
4. Describe similarities and differences of middle level programs and instructional practices based on grade level organizational structure and other demographic data
5. Describe programs and leaders of schools that are restructuring successfully
6. Contrast the programs and leadership of successful restructuring schools with those of typical middle level schools
7. Identify trends in middle level education and leadership that will assist educators in the implementation of quality middle level schools for the next century.

The study was undertaken in two major phases. This report, representing Phase I, presents survey data collected in the 1991–92 school year. When appropriate, these data have been contrasted with other national studies of middle level education. The following chronological list of cited studies/reports is provided to assist the reader.

- 1966—National Association of Secondary School Principals' initial study of junior high school leaders and programs reported in *The Junior High Principalship*, Donald A. Rock and John K. Hemphill.
- 1968—study of middle school programs reported in *The Emergent Middle School*, William M. Alexander, Emmett I. Williams, Mary Compton, Vynce A. Hines, Dan Prescott, and Ronald Kealy.
- 1978—study of middle school programs reported in *The Middle School in Transition*, Kenneth Brooks and Francine Edwards.
- 1981—National Association of Secondary School Principals' study of middle level leaders

and programs, reported in *The Middle Level Principalship: Volume 1, A Survey of Middle Level Principals and Programs,* Jerry W. Valentine, Donald C. Clark, Neal C. Nickerson, Jr., and James W. Keefe.

- 1989—Study of middle level programs, reported in *Earmarks of Schools in the Middle: A Research Report,* William M. Alexander and C. Kenneth McEwin.

- 1990—Study of middle level programs by the Center for Research on Elementary and Middle Schools reported in *Education in the Middle Grades: National Practices and Trends,* Joyce L. Epstein and Douglas J. Mac Iver.

Phase II of this study will be described in a second volume, entitled *Leadership in Successful Restructuring Middle Level Schools.* That study will include comprehensive assessment data on some 50 schools and survey information that can be compared with the national sample data presented in this report. In addition, a case study analysis will be conducted of the leadership characteristics and programs in 10 of the 50 schools.

Instrumentation

Phase I survey items collected longitudinal data from principals, assistant principals, and leadership team members for comparison with previous national surveys of these groups. The items were designed to reflect the current literature and best practice in middle level schools on the themes of leadership, programs, and issues/trends. The items were reviewed by a steering committee of practitioners in middle level education. One hundred three items were selected for the principalship and school program survey. Sixty-one items were chosen for the assistant principalship survey, 45 items for the leadership team member survey. Because of the number of items needed from principals, two survey forms were developed. Form A consisted of 57 questions, and Form B had 61 questions. Both forms had 15 common items. The instrument was field tested in the fall of 1991, and data were collected in the winter of 1991–92.

Population and Sample

In the 1991–92 school year, there were approximately 12,100 middle level schools in the United States. A middle level school was defined in this study as one composed of any grade or grade combination between grades 5 and 9. The more typical grade configurations of 6–7–8, 7–8, and 7–8–9, as well as more atypical patterns such as 5–6, 8–9, 6–7, etc., were included in the population. A systematic and stratified sample of 2,000 middle level schools was selected from the population. This sample size (16.5 percent), proportionate by grade pattern, exceeded standard random sampling requirements for the population. The sample was composed of 40 percent 6–7–8 schools, 24 percent 7–8 schools, 19 percent 7–8–9 schools, 11 percent 5–6–7–8 schools, and 6 percent other patterns.

The principals of the selected schools were mailed an introductory letter explaining the study and requesting participation. Survey instruments for the principal, an assistant principal, and a leadership team member were included in the packet. Half the principals (1,000) received Principal Survey Form A, and half (1,000) received Principal Survey Form B. Principals were asked to give the Assistant Principal Survey to their chief assistant (if they had one) and to a member of their leadership team (if they had one, either formal or informal). A leadership team member was defined as a "teacher who has been designated by the principal to assist in the leadership operation of the school."

From the sample of 2,000 schools, 570 principals (29 percent) provided usable returns. This response number was smaller than in past surveys but large enough to justify confidence that the returns were representative of the population. Basic demographic items for the first 50 and last 50 respondents were tested and not found to be significantly different. (Late respondents are typically similar to nonrespondents.)

Of the 570 principals who responded, 439 (77 percent) had an assistant principal. If this percentage were extrapolated to the entire sample of 2,000, approximately 1,400 schools had assistant principals. Twenty-nine percent of the schools with assistants provided usable returns (404).

Sixty-eight percent of the responding principals reported a leadership team in their schools. If the number of respondents with teams were extrapolated to the total sample, approximately 1,360 schools had leadership teams. From the responding schools, 411 leadership team members provided usable responses, a 30 percent rate of return. In all, 1,385 middle level educators invested up to two hours each to complete the surveys.

Description of the Sample

The schools in the study represented a broad cross section of middle level grade organizational structures. Data in this report have regularly been presented by grade patterns so that readers could perceive the relationship of organization to other issues. Of the respondents, 50 percent represented 6–7–8 grade patterns; 12 percent were 5–6–7–8; 18 percent, 7–8; 15 percent, 7–8–9; and 5 percent, other combinations. This response distribution was generally similar to the distribution of schools in the sampling frame, but 6–8 schools were overrepresented by 10 percent and 7–8 and 7–9 schools underrepresented by a similar amount.

The schools in the study were representative of each geographic region of the United States. Ten percent were from the New England region, 17 percent from the Mid-Atlantic, 17 percent from the South, 31 percent from the Midwest, 9 percent from the Southwest, 5 percent from the Rocky Mountains, and 11 percent from the Far West, including Alaska and Hawaii.

The populations of the communities in the sample were also representative of communities across the United States. Large cities of 150,000 or more persons represented 13 percent of the schools in the study, with related suburbs comprising another 25 percent. Sixteen percent of the schools were from communities of 25,000 to 149,999, and 21 percent from those of 5,000 to 24,999. Small towns and rural areas under 5,000 population constituted 26 percent of the respondents.

Each principal was asked to indicate the number of students enrolled in the school. Three percent enrolled fewer than 200 students. Nineteen percent had 200 to 399 students; 27 percent, from 400 to 599 students; 23 percent, from 600 to 799 students; 12 percent, from 800 to 999 students; 9 percent, from 1,000 to 1,199 students; 4 percent, from 1,200 to 1,399 students; and only 3 percent enrolled 1,400 or more students.

Principals were asked to indicate, exclusive of capital outlay, the per pupil expenditure of their schools. Twenty-three percent reported less than $2,500, 34 percent from $2,500 to $3,499, 24 percent from $3,500 to $4,499, and 19 percent reported $4,500 or more.

These demographic data offered another basis for analyzing responses throughout the study.

Organization of the Report

This report presents more than just an item-by-item response to the survey questions. Relationships between questions and among respondents have been discussed. Responses have been compared by demographic and other control variables such as grade patterns and gender. Responses also have been contrasted with data from other studies.

The chapters of the report are organized thematically to describe Personal and Professional Characteristics, School Leadership, Educational Programs, Issues and Trends, and Leadership Profiles. Data in these chapters provide a frame of reference for viewing contemporary leaders, practices, and issues. The data also provide a longitudinal perspective for comparisons with previous and future studies of middle level leaders and programs.

The Steering Committee and the Research Team believe that the principal and the school leadership team are the most critical elements in the evolution of quality school programs. Schools must constantly strive for improvement; they must be constantly restructuring. Leadership efforts have been described in this report that can support successful restructuring. From the baseline data of the report, conclusions can be drawn about numerous practices and issues in middle level education. It will be the continuing challenge of scholars and practitioners to use these data to nourish and support even more successful schools for pre and early adolescents.

Chapter 1

Personal/Professional Characteristics

Examining middle level leadership has been a major priority of the National Association of Secondary School Principals for the last quarter of a century. In sponsoring three national middle level studies (1966, 1981–83, and 1992–94), NASSP has documented leadership issues and trends in middle level schools during the dramatic period of change from a junior high school format to the current middle school format.

The first NASSP middle level study, conducted in 1966, paralleled the efforts of middle school advocates William Alexander and Donald Eichhorn, who were beginning their efforts to clarify the goals and purposes of middle level schools. Data from that initial NASSP study of the junior high school principalship has become the baseline for assessing current programs and practices.

Middle level principals and programs were the focus of Phase I of NASSP's second major study; the effective middle level principalship was the subject of Phase II. That two-part study (1981–83) surveyed middle level principals throughout the United States, including on-site visits to successful middle level schools.

The current study represents NASSP's continuing commitment to middle level research. The expansion of the study to include assistant principals and leadership team members in addition to principals recognizes changing leadership patterns and adds a new dimension to the study of leadership in middle level education.

The three NASSP studies trace the development of middle level schools and leaders over the past quarter-century and suggest some clues about the direction of middle level education in this decade and beyond. In the first chapter of this current study, we will review the personal and professional characteristics of our subjects, including the gender and age distributions, their ethnicity, professional experience, academic preparation, administrative status and welfare, career plans, and several organizational variables that describe their schools.

Personal Factors

❏ Distribution of School Leaders by Gender

A dramatic increase in the percentage of women middle level principals has taken place in the last three decades. Data from this study (Table 1.1) indicated that 20 percent of the middle level principals in 1992 were women, up considerably from the 1981 study (6 percent), and the 1966 study (4 percent). Women were also well represented in other leadership positions, with more than one-third serving as assistant principals and two-thirds holding memberships on school leadership teams.

TABLE 1.1

Gender of School Leaders

	1992 Principals	1992 Assistant Principals	1992 Team Members	1981 Principals	1966 Principals
Male	80	65	34	94	96
Female	20	35	66	6	4

From 1981 to 1992, the percentage of female principals increased in *each* of the various middle level school grade configurations (Table 1.2). The most dramatic increase was in schools with atypical grade combinations, such as 6–7, or single grade 7 or 8. The 7–8 combination was the only grade pattern in which the percentage of female principals did not at least double during those years.

TABLE 1.2

Principal Gender by Grade Level

	All Schools		6–7–8		5–6–7–8		7–8		7–8–9		Other	
	1981	1992	1981	1992	1981	1992	1981	1992	1981	1992	1981	1992
Female	6	20	8	22	9	20	8	11	5	19	4	32
Male	94	80	92	78	91	80	92	89	95	81	96	68

Age

Contemporary middle level principals appear to be slightly older than their counterparts of 1966 and 1981 (Table 1.3). Between 1966 and 1981, the percentage of principals in the 45–54 age bracket increased from 31 to 42 percent. By 1992, the figure was 48 percent. From 1966 to 1992, there was a 16 percent decrease in the number of principals in their 30s and a 22 percent increase of those in their 40s. The percentages for those in their 50s remained fairly constant. These patterns were also similar for elementary and high school principals.

Age	1992			1981	1966	1988	1978	1965	1989	1979
	Middle Level Prin.	Middle Level AP	Team Members	Middle Level Prin.	Junior High Prin.	Senior High Prin.	Senior High AP	Senior High Prin.	Senior High Prin.	Elem. Prin.	Elem. Prin.
29	1	2	4	1	2	0	1	1	4	5	2
30–34	2	6	10	8	8	3	7	8	12	0	12
35–39	9	14	18	15	19	16	21	16	18	16	15
40–44	26	33	28	18	18	24	26	22	16	21	17
45–49	29	24	25	21	15	21	19	22	15	19	20
50–54	19	14	10	21	16	19	16	19	15	20	19
55–59	12	6	4	11	14	11	8	8	12	14	11
60	3	2	1	5	8	5	3	5	8	5	6

TABLE 1.3

Age of School Leaders

The authors of the 1981 middle level report speculated that retrenchment in the job market and more demanding requirements in many states for principal certification contributed to the aging cohort of building principals. These may also be contributing factors in 1992. Another factor may be the dramatic increase in the quantity and quality of services provided to principals in the 1980s by their professional associations and other agencies. Associations experienced unprecedented membership growth in that decade. Association services to members may have contributed to increased job satisfaction, security, and professional growth. Various programs at the state and national levels also reflected a more positive image of the principal. These factors undoubtedly make the principalship a more desirable, rewarding, and long-term career.

Middle level assistant principals are younger than the principals. Only 11 percent of the principals were younger than 40, contrasted with 20 percent of their assistants. Thirty-four percent of the principals were in their 50s, but only 22 percent of the assistants. The ages of middle level leadership team members were similar to those of assistant principals.

❑ Ethnicity

In 1992, approximately 10 percent of middle level principals identified themselves as non-white, compared with 8 percent in 1981. The 1988 high school study reported approximately 6 percent non-white principals; the 1989 elementary data showed approximately 10 percent non-white (Table 1.4).

TABLE 1.4

Ethnicity of School Leaders

	1992			1981	1966	1988		1978	1989	1979
	Middle Level Prin.	Middle Level AP	Team Members	Middle Level Prin.	Junior High Prin.	Senior High Prin.	Senior High AP	Senior High Prin.	Elem. Prin.	Elem. Prin.
White	90	86	92	92	Data not avail-able	94	89	96	89	91
Black	6	9	5	6		4	10	3	4	6
Hispanic American	2	3	1	1		2	2	1	4	1
Indian	< 1	< 1	< 1	< 1		< 1	< 1	< 1	2	2
Asian	1	< 1	< 1	< 1		< 1	< 1	< 1	0	< 1
Other	1	< 1	< 1	< 1		< 1	< 1	< 1	< 1	< 1

Table 1.5 shows that, as in 1981, the incidence of non-white female principals was higher than that of males. In 1981, 8 percent of non-white principals were male, but 17 percent were female. In 1992, the percentage of non-white males remained the same, but non-white females dropped by 2 percent. From 1981 to 1992, the percentage of black and American Indian female principals decreased while the percentage of Hispanic and Asian female principals increased slightly.

TABLE 1.5

Ethnicity of Middle Level Principals by Gender

	White	Black	Chicano Hispanic	American Indian	Asian	Other
1981						
Male	92	6	1	< 1	< 1	< 1
Female	83	12	2	2	1	0
1992						
Male	92	5	2	< 1	< 1	< 1
Female	85	9	4	0	2	0

In cities of more than 150,000 population, 33 percent of the principals were non-white, an increase of 14 percent since 1981 (Table 1.6). This increase was due primarily to greater percentages of Hispanic and Asian principals.

TABLE 1.6

Ethnicity by Community Population

Ethnicity	All Schools	150,000+	Suburban	25,000–149,999	5,000–24,999	Rural
White						
1981	92	81	94	90	96	94
1992	90	67	95	94	92	91
Black						
1981	6	18	3	7	3	5
1992	6	19	3	4	5	5
Hispanic						
1981	1	1	1	2	0	1
1992	2	7	1	1	3	3
American Indian						
1981	< 1	0	1	1	< 1	< 1
1992	< 1	0	1	0	0	1
Asian						
1981	< 1	< 1	< 1	0	0	0
1992	< 1	5	0	1	0	0
Other						
1981	< 1	0	1	1	1	1
1992	< 1	2	0	0	0	0

Professional Factors

❑ Age at Appointment to First Principalship/Assistant Principalship

Half the 1981 middle level principals were 34 years of age or younger when they first entered the principalship. By 1992, the percentage had dropped to 38 (Table 1.7). In 1965, 61 percent were selected for a first principalship in senior high schools before age 34; it was 50 percent in 1978, and 44 percent in 1988. For elementary principals, the number beginning in the principalship before the age of 34 dropped from 59 percent in 1979 to 56 percent in 1989. At all levels, those entering the principalship are older than their counterparts in the earlier studies.

Among assistant principals, only about 25 percent were first appointed at age 34 or younger. On the average, the age at which assistant principals were first appointed was older than that for principals. This is probably a system artifact. Principals with a first appointment at an early age are usually assigned to relatively small schools. Assistants are needed in larger schools, where appointments go to those with more experience.

TABLE 1.7
Age at First Appointment to the Principalship/Assistant Principalship

Age	1992	1981	1988	1978	1965	1989	1979
	Middle Level Prin.	Middle Level AP	Middle Level Prin.	Senior High Prin.	Senior High Prin.	Senior High Prin.	Elem. Prin.	Elem. Prin.
24 or less	1	< 1						
25–29	15	9	19	14	22	34	26	} 59
30–34	22	16	31	30	28	27	30	
35–39	26	28	22	27	24	18	24	} 38
40–44	22	29	18	17	15	11	10	
45–49	10	13	6	9	7	6	7	} 3
50–54	4	5	6	3	3	3	} 3	
55 or older	0	< 1	1	1	0	1		

❑ Previous Experience

The number of years of teaching experience for principals has changed little since 1981 (Table 1.8). When analyzed by gender, however, contemporary female principals have taught noticeably more years than their male counterparts. Female principals of today have more teaching experience than their counterparts of 1981 and considerably more than their male counterparts of today.

TABLE 1.8
Principal Years of Teaching Experience Prior to Present Position by Gender

	1981			1992		
	Total	Male	Female	Total	Male	Female
3 or fewer	8	7	4	8	9	5
4–9	49	50	33	40	43	25
10 or more	43	43	63	52	48	70

Table 1.9 shows that 36 percent of today's principals came to that position from a middle level assistant principalship. This represents an increase of 7 percent since 1981, and a striking 16 percent increase when compared with 1966. If this percentage is combined with those coming from middle level teaching, 45 percent of middle level principals came directly from another position in a middle level school. Approximately one-third of the respondents came from a high school position. Only 16 percent came to the middle level principalship from elementary teaching or administrative positions.

In 1966, 1981, and 1992, more middle level principals moved to their principalships from the assistant principalship than from teaching positions.

TABLE 1.9

Last Position Held Prior to the Principalship

| | 1992 | | 1981 | 1966 |
	Principals	Assistant Principals	Principals	Principals
Elementary Teacher	2	8	2	*
Middle Level Teacher	9	39	12	*
High School Teacher	3	14	8	13
Elementary Assistant Principal	2	1	2	1
Middle Level Assistant Principal	36	1	29	20
High School Assistant Principal	20	6	18	11
Elementary Principal	12	3	12	21
High School Principal	7	2	7	6
Guidance Counselor	1	1	2	*
Central Office Administrator	2	6	3	*
College Instructor/Administrator	1	3	*	*
Other	6	16	5	10
Elementary/Junior High Teacher	*	*	*	18

*Data not available

Fifty-one percent of the principals and 44 percent of the assistant principals reported one or more years of experience as an athletic coach (Table 1.10). Fewer than 25 percent have held athletic administrative positions. The implication here is that a decreasing number of middle level principals came from professional coaching backgrounds. Sixty-two percent of both principals and assistants reported experience as department chairpersons or team leaders.

Personal/Professional Characteristics

TABLE 1.10

Positions in Which Principals/Assistant Principals Have Had One Full Year
or More of Experience

	Principals	Assistant Principals
Athletic Coach	51	44
Athletic Director	23	19
Counselor/Guidance Position	16	12
Dean or Registrar	10	4
Department Chairperson	37	39
Team Leader	25	23
Dean of Studies	*	< 1
Activities Director	*	17
Dean of Students	*	8

❑ Years in Leadership Positions

Shifts in the number of years principals have served in that position have not been significant over the three reporting periods. The greatest difference occurs in the 10 to 14-year category, with a 6 percent drop since 1981 (Table 1.11).

The 1992 assistant principals have been in their positions fewer years than the principals, with 76 percent reporting seven years or fewer of administrative experience, compared with 47 percent reporting among the principals.

TABLE 1.11

Years as Principal/Assistant Principal, Including This Year

	1992		1981	1966
Years	Principals	Asst. Prin.	Principals	Principals
1	6	15	7	6
2–3	16	30	12	14
4–5	13	18	10	14
6–7	12	13	13	11
8–9	8	6	11	11
10–14	16	8	22	18
15–19	15	79	13	11
20–24	9	2	8	6
25	5	1	4	9

❏ Years in Present School

Forty-six percent of middle level principals indicated (Table 1.12) that they were in the first three years of their present assignment, an increase of 12 percent since 1981. In 1988, at the high school level, 38 percent reported tenure of three years or fewer. Apparently, a substantial turnover has occurred in middle level principalships in recent years.

For middle level assistant principals, 59 percent are still in the first three years of their present position, 13 percent more than the principals in the same category. Since team leadership is a relatively new management strategy, it is not surprising that 66 percent of team members reported being in the first three years of that role.

TABLE 1.12

Years as Principal/Assistant Principal/Leadership Team Member in Present School

Years	1992	1981	1966	1988	1978	1965		
	Middle Level Prin.	Middle Level AP	Middle Level Team Members	Middle Level Prin.	Junior High Prin.	High School Prin.	High School Prin.	High School Prin.
1	15	20	15	13	13	15	12	16
2	16	23	31	12	14	13	13	14
3	15	16	20	9	12	10	11	12
4–5	15	17	9	16	20	15	19	18
6–8	11	10	8	19	18	17	21	15
9–11	10	6	8	12	11	11	11	9
12–14	5	3	6	8	4	8	6	5
15–17	6	2	3	6	3	6	NA	NA
15 or more	NA	NA	NA	NA	NA	12	6	11
18 or more	7	3	1	5	5	6	NA	NA

❏ Undergraduate Study

Social studies continues to be the major area of undergraduate study for middle level principals, with 26 percent reporting that major in 1992 (22 percent in 1981). Social studies was also the primary area of preparation for assistant principals. Physical education and elementary education were also frequently reported (Table 1.13). It is not surprising that fewer than 1 percent of the principals cited middle level education as their major area of preparation. That figure will undoubtedly change as colleges and universities continue to add middle level specialization at both the undergraduate and graduate levels.

TABLE 1.13

Major Area of Undergraduate Study

| Area | 1992 | | 1981 | 1966 |
	Principals	Assistant Principals	Principals	Principals
Mathematics	5	8	7	*
Phys. or Biol. Science	9	6	11	15
Social Science	26	21	22	1
Humanities [a]	9	13	7	24
Physical Ed.	17	12	15	12
Business	2	4	5	5
Fine Arts	4	3	3	3
Voc/Tech [b]	3	3	5	*
Elementary Ed.	15	18	11	*
Secondary Ed. [c]	5	5	11	*
Middle Level Education	< 1	< 1	*	*
Other	4	6	4	6

[a]   Literature, Language, etc.
[b]   Home Economics, Industrial Arts, etc.
[c]   Other than Physical Education
*   Data Not Available

❏ Graduate Study

The field of educational administration/supervision was the major area of graduate study for approximately three-fourths of the middle level principals in each of the NASSP studies: 73 percent in 1992, 75 percent in 1981, and 78 percent in 1966. The percentage of curriculum and instruction majors increased slightly from 1981 to 1992 (Table 1.14). Middle level assistant principals reported more preparation in curriculum and instruction than did principals.

❏ Highest Degree Earned

The master's degree with additional credits of graduate study remains normative for middle level principals, assistant principals, and leadership team members (Table 1.15). Principals with educational specialist/6-year degrees increased from 10 percent in 1981, to 17 percent in 1992. The percentage of principals who have completed all the coursework for, or earned the doctorate, nearly doubled from 1966 (11 percent), to 1992 (20 percent). Nine percent of assistants and 3 percent of leadership team members reported doctoral-level study.

Clearly, higher levels of graduate preparation have been a consistent pattern for the past 25 years.

TABLE 1.14

Major Field of Graduate Study

Major Field: Graduate	1992		1981	1966
	Principals	Assistant Principals	Principals	Principals
Ed. Admin./Supervision	73	68	75	78
Secondary Educ./C&I	8	9	6	9
Middle Level Ed./C&I	< 1	*	*	*
Elementary Ed./C&I	4	5	1	*
Guidance/ Counseling	5	6	5	*
Physical Education	1	1	2	2
Other Ed. Specialties	2	3	2	5
Humanities, Social Sciences & Fine Arts	3	1	3	3
Math/Sciences	< 1	2	4	1
Business	0	1	< 1	0
Other	2	4	1	1
No Graduate Study	< 1	< 1	1	1

* Data Not Available

TABLE 1.15

Highest Degree Earned

Degree	1992			1981	1966
	Principals	Assistant Principals	Team Members	Principals	Principals
Less than Bachelor's	0	0	< 1	*	0
Bachelor's	< 1	1	29	1	6
Master's in Education	15	24	20	23	33
Master's NOT in Ed.	< 1	< 1	2	1	2
Master's +	49	47	37	49	47
Ed. Specialist 6 years	16	16	7	10	*
Master's + All Course-work for Doctorate	9	4	1	7	7
Doctor of Ed.	9	3	< 1	5	3
Doctor of Philosophy	2	2	0	3	1
Other	0	3	3	1	1

* Data not available

Personal/Professional Characteristics

Female middle level principals continue to be better prepared academically than their male counterparts (Table 1.16). More than half the females have earned the specialist or doctoral degree, contrasted with less than one-third the males. This widens a trend from 1981.

The increase in preparation level of middle level administrators is a promising trend. The increase may reflect more stringent requirements for administrative licensing in some states, but it is not unreasonable to speculate that greater respectability for a "middle level of education" has prompted better prepared principals to remain in middle level schools rather than to seek other levels of service.

TABLE 1.16
Highest Degree Earned, by Gender

Degree	1992		1981	
	Male	Female	Male	Female
Bachelor's Degree	< 1	0	1	4
Master's Degree	67	46	81	65
Specialist's Degree	23	37	10	11
Doctorate	9	17	7	18
Other	0	0	1	2

❏ Administrative Certification

The most significant finding reported in Table 1.17 is the doubling, since 1981, of the percentage of principals with middle level administrative certification. Equally satisfying is the fact that 14 percent of assistant principals are certificated at the middle level.

TABLE 1.17
Principal/Assistant Principal Administrative Certification

Certification	1992		1981
	Principals	Assistant Principals	Principals
Secondary	56	50	66
Middle	16	14	8
Elementary	8	10	7
No Principal Certification	1	12	6
Other	19	15	13

Table 1.18 shows that secondary certification continues to be the predominant pathway for middle level administrators, but the percentage has decreased 10 percent since 1981. The grade level pattern reporting more middle level-certificated principals and the greatest increase since 1981 was 6–7–8, the most common middle level configuration. The highest percentage of secondary-certificated administrators was reported for the 7–8–9 grade pattern, the traditional junior high school configuration.

TABLE 1.18

Principal Administrative Certification by Grade Level

	All Schools		6–7–8		5–6–7–8		7–8		7–8–9		Others	
Certification	'81	'92	'81	'92	'81	'92	'81	'92	'81	'92	'81	'92
Secondary	66	56	51	52	30	42	61	42	77	79	65	31
Middle	8	16	10	21	9	16	8	16	7	10	11	15
Elementary	7	8	14	7	22	20	9	20	2	0	9	8
None	6	2	8	1	14	3	8	3	4	3	6	8
Other	13	19	17	19	25	19	14	19	10	8	9	38

❑ Salary and Tenure

The most common contractual period for both principals and assistant principals is 12 months, with 64 percent of the principals and 37 percent of the assistants so reporting (Table 1.19). Eighty-seven percent of the principals and 58 percent of the assistants reported contracts of at least 11 months. The majority of both principals and assistant principals have single-year contracts (Table 1.20).

TABLE 1.19

Length of Salary Contract

	1992		1981
Contract Length	Principals	Assistant Principals	Principals
12 months	64	37	47
11 1/2 months	3	1	< 1
11 months	20	20	28
10 1/2 months	7	17	15
10 months	6	21	10
9 1/2 months	0	3	< 1
9 months	< 1	1	0

TABLE 1.20

Is Contract Multi-Year?

Multi-Year	Principals	Assistant Principals
No	56	65
Yes-Two Year	22	17
Yes-Three Year	15	14
Yes-More than Three Years	7	3

Two-thirds of the principals were without tenure as principal in 1992, down 1 percent from 1981. Approximately three-fourths of assistant principals lacked position tenure (Table 1.21).

TABLE 1.21

Tenure as a Principal/Assistant Principal

Tenure	1992		1981	1966
	Principals	Assistant Principals	Principals	Principals
Yes	33	23	35	45
No	67	77	65	55

❑ Salary and Benefits

In 1992, 82 percent of the middle level principals reported a salary of more than $45,000 (Table 1.22). This offers an interesting contrast with the 1981 study, when fewer than 1 percent of the principals reported a salary greater than that amount. Even a majority of current middle level assistant principals reported salaries above $45,000. As recently as 1988, only 44 percent of high school principals earned more than $45,000. Salary levels for middle level administrators have accelerated significantly in the past five years, probably mirroring the wider attempts of the school restructuring movement to raise teacher salaries to more competitive levels.

More than half the responding principals and assistant principals indicated that their salaries were determined by group or individual negotiations. The only significant shift in prevailing policy was a decline in the use of teacher schedules to determine administrative salaries (Table 1.23).

TABLE 1.22

Annual Salary

Salary	1992 Middle Level Prin.	1992 Middle Level AP	1981 Middle Level Prin.	1988 High School Prin.	1988 High School AP	1987 Elem. Prin.
< 25,000	NA	NA	NA	4	8	
25,000–29,999	< 1	2	64	5	9	26.3
30,000–34,999	< 1	7	26	12	19	
35,000–39,999	6	15	8	14	23	24.7
40,000–44,999	11	23	2	19	22	21.2
45,000–49,999	18	14	< 1	16	9	16.6
50,000 or more						11.3
50,000–54,999	16	19	NA	15	6	11.3**
55,000 or more					3	
55,000–59,999	14	8	NA	6	3*	
60,000				7		
60,000–64,999	15	7	NA	NA		
65,000–69,999	9	3	NA	NA		
70,000	10	3	NA	NA		

* actually $55,000 or more
** actually $50,000 or more

TABLE 1.23

Basis for Salary Determination

Basis	1992 Principals	1992 Asst. Prin.	1981 Principals
Percent of Step in Teacher Salary Sched.	7	4	15
Teacher Salary + Increment	14	20	15
Administrative Negotiations	41	47	36
Individual Negotiations	10	4	6
Non-Negotiable Administrative Sched.	22	21	23
N/A-Religious Order	< 1	< 1	1
Other	6	3	4

Personal/Professional Characteristics

Table 1.24 confirms a long-standing trend that principals in larger communities earn more than those in smaller communities. Eleven percent of the principals in communities of 150,000 or more, 24 percent of the suburban principals, and 14 percent of those in mid-size cities, earned $70,000 or more. In small cities and rural communities, most principals earned less than $50,000.

TABLE 1.24

Middle Level Principal Salaries by Community Type

	All Schools	150,000 or more	Suburb	25,000 to 149,999	5,000 to 24,000	Rural
35,000	1	0	2	0	3	0
35,000–39,999	6	4	0	0	5	16
40,000–44,999	11	0	3	11	20	21
45,000–49,999	18	8	5	19	28	33
50,000–54,999	16	27	11	13	18	15
55,000–59,999	14	19	13	16	8	11
60,000–64,999	15	23	26	13	10	2
65,000–69,999	9	8	16	11	3	2
70,000 +	10	11	24	14	5	0
N/A	1	0	0	3	0	0

Medical insurance was received as a benefit by three-fourths of all the respondents. Approximately two-thirds also received dental and life insurance coverage. An auto/mileage allowance was provided for 55 percent of the principals and for 37 percent of the assistants. Other benefits are summarized in Table 1.25.

TABLE 1.25

Fringe Benefits Received in Addition to Salary

Benefit	Principals	Asst. Prin.
Medical Insurance	79	76
Dental Insurance	65	64
Life Insurance	64	66
Auto/Mileage Allowance	55	37
College Tuition for Self	22	14
Expense Account	11	3
Meals	8	3
No Fringe Benefits	< 1	6
Tuition for Dependents (Non-public)	< 1	< 1
Housing/Equivalent Subsidy	< 1	< 1

❑ Career Plans

Fifty percent of the 1992 middle level principals plan to remain in their present positions for the next three to five years (Table 1.26). This is approximately the same percentage as in 1966, but 13 percent higher than in 1981. The increase over the last 12 years may be due, at least in part, to the improved image of and attention given to middle level schools and continuing improvement in job satisfaction and rewards. Many 1981 respondents functioned during the difficult years of the late '60s and early '70s and were understandably considering a change. Perhaps an even more significant change from 1981 to 1992 was the 20 percent drop in the percentage of principals seeking the superintendency. Apparently, the principalship is much more attractive than the superintendency to many administrators today.

TABLE 1.26

Middle Level Principals' Career Plans for the Next Three to Five Years

Career Plans	1992	1981	1966
Remain in Present Position	50	37	51
Retirement	14	*	*
Seek Superintendency	6	26	16
Central Office Other than Superintendent	15	*	*
Different M.L. Principalship	2	1	*
Elementary Principalship	1	2	*
High School Principalship	3	7	9
Junior College or University	< 1	2	8
State Department or Other Education Agency	< 1	2	*
Return to Full-Time Teaching	0	0	0
Outside Field of Education	1	*	17
Undecided	6	18	*

* Data not available

It is in the best interest of middle level education for good principals to stay in that position. However, it is somewhat discouraging to see the steady drop in the percentage contemplating a move to a college or university position (currently less than 1 percent). With the ever-growing need for graduate and undergraduate programs in middle level education, some of the most effective principals could make a significant contribution by moving to the collegiate level. The indications are that this is not likely to happen. Economic factors are involved. In any event, the placement of more principals in adjunct or visiting professor positions would be a welcome and positive move.

Personal/Professional Characteristics

❏ Average Daily Attendance

Table 1.27 illustrates the improvements in school average daily attendance since 1981. In 1992, 90 percent of the students were in attendance at least 90 percent of the time. That level of attendance represents an outstanding 11 percent increase since 1981. It seems fair to attribute some of that improvement to the move toward middle school grade patterns, programs, and philosophy as schools became more client-centered.

TABLE 1.27

Percent of Average Daily Attendance for Those Enrolled

	1992 Principals	1981 Principals
70 percent or less	1	3
81–90 percent	9	18
91–95 percent	48	60
96 percent or more	42	19

❏ Per Pupil Expenditure

It is hardly surprising that the highest per pupil expenditure on the 1966 and 1981 surveys did not even constitute the lowest step in 1992. Approximately half the 1992 schools reported per-pupil costs between $2,500 and $3,999 (Table 1.28). The highest figure on the 1966 survey was $700 or more; $1,800 or more in 1981. The current figure frequently reported in other surveys for average per pupil expenditure is $5,500. Only 12 percent of the schools in this study expended in excess of $5,000.

TABLE 1.28

Average Per Pupil Expenditure

1992		1981		1966	
Less than $2,000	11	Less than $1,200	38	Less than $30	2
$2,000–$2,499	12	$1,200–$1,799	43	$30–$99	2
$2,500–$2,999	12	$1,800 or more	19	$100–$199	2
$3,000–$3,499	22			$200–$299	12
$3,500–$3,999	13			$300–$399	27
$4,000–$4,499	11			$400–$499	25
$4,500–$4,999	7			$500–599	12
$5,000 or more	12			$600–$699	5
				$700 or more	3
				No Response	10

❑ Organizational Grade Patterns

The continuing decline of the 7–8–9 junior high grade level configuration is reinforced in this study (Table 1.29). Fifteen percent of the respondents reported schools with grades 7–8–9, a drop of 27 percentage points from 1981 (42 percent), and down 52 percent from the 1966 study (67 percent).

This steady decline in schools surveyed parallels the actual number of schools as reported by governmental and professional organizations. Equally dramatic has been the steady increase of 6–7–8 schools, from 5 percent in 1966 to 50 percent in 1992. Demographic considerations, of course, play a part in these and other school reorganizations.

Table 1.29 also shows an increase in the 5–6–7–8 grade pattern. Some educators are (once again) recommending this configuration. One rationale is that the onset of puberty occurs for many youngsters near or during the sixth grade, the same grade in which they must adjust to a new school, new teachers, friends, programs, etc. Beginning middle level schooling at the fifth grade, these educators suggest, would enable students to make those adjustments before they must deal with the challenges of puberty. Whether this recommendation will become a trend remains to be seen.

TABLE 1.29			
Grades Included in Middle Level School			
	1992	1981	1966
7–8–9	15	42	67
6–7–8	50	15	5
5–6–7	< 1	< 1	*
5–6–7–8	12	4	*
6–7–8–9	< 1	< 1	1
5–6	< 1	< 1	*
6–7	1	< 1	*
7–8	18	31	20
8–9	< 1	3	*
Other	2	3	7

Further data on reorganization trends will be found in Table 1.30. Thirty-three percent of reporting schools have maintained their present grade pattern for five years or fewer; 54 percent have changed the pattern in the past 10 years. This volume of change primarily represents the major decrease in the 7–8–9 pattern and the corresponding increase in the 6–7–8 pattern.

Personal/Professional Characteristics

TABLE 1.30

Number of Years School Has Operated Under Current Grade
Level Configuration

	1992	1981
1 Year	6	NA
5 Years	27	19
6–10 Years	21	26
11–15 Years	14	19
16–20 Years	11	14
21 Years +	21	22

❏ Regional Accreditation

Principals were asked whether their schools were accredited by a regional accrediting association. A modest increase has occurred in the percentages of middle level schools accredited since 1981 (Table 1.31).

TABLE 1.31

Is School Accredited by a Regional Accrediting Association?

	1992	1981
Yes	54	48
No	46	52

❏ Leadership Team Members

Principals were asked to report the titles of members of their middle level school leadership teams. Thirty-five percent of the members were simply characterized as teachers, with 23 percent identified as team leaders. Table 32 also shows that 17 percent of these team members are called department chairpersons.

TABLE 1.32

Official Title of Leadership Team Members　,

Title	1992	Title	1992
Teacher	35	House Leader	1
Department Chair	17	Dean	2
Team Leader	23	Coordinator	6
Administrative Intern	1	Other	14
Master Teacher	1		

Exactly half the reporting leadership team members have served in their present schools for a period of 3 to 11 years. An additional 10 percent have served 12 to 14 years. Twenty-four percent have 18 or more years of service (Table 1.33)

The majority of team members have considerable experience, both in their present schools and elsewhere. Eighty-one percent have served as a teacher for 10 or more years (Table 1.34).

TABLE 1.33

Years Leadership Team Member Worked as Educator in Present School, Including This Year

Number of Years	1992	Number of Years	1992
1	1	9–11	15
2	6	12–14	10
3	7	15–17	9
4–5	14	18 or More	24
6–8	14		

TABLE 1.34

Number of Years Leadership Team Members Served as a Teacher, Including This Year

Number of Years	1992	Number of Years	1992
1	1	10–14	21
2–3	2	15–19	25
4–5	5	20–24	24
6–7	7	25 or More	11
8–9	5		

Leadership team members were also asked about the number of years they taught in their schools before serving as a leadership team member (Table 1.35). The majority had taught between 4 and 15 years before being selected. Most have served as team members for fewer than 5 years (Table 1.36).

Personal/Professional Characteristics

TABLE 1.35

Number of Years Taught Before Serving as a Leadership Team Member

Number of Years	1992	Number of Years	1992
None	6	10–14	19
1	6	15–19	15
2–3	15	20–24	5
4–6	18	25 or More	2
7–9	13		

TABLE 1.36

Number of Years Contributed to Operation of School as a Leadership Team Member

Number of Years	1992	Number of Years	1992
1	15	10–14	8
2–3	31	15–19	6
4–5	20	20–24	2
6–7	9	25 or More	1
8–9	8		

Sixty-eight percent of leadership team members represented academic core teaching areas of math, science, language arts, and social studies (Table 1.37). These areas demand the largest block of teachers in most schools, and logically were represented more heavily on leadership teams.

TABLE 1.37

Teaching Area of Leadership Team Members

Teaching Area	1992
Mathematics	16
Physical or Biological Science	10
Social Sciences (sociology, history, etc.)	17
Humanities (literature, languages, etc.)	25
Physical Education	3
Business	1
Fine Arts	2
Voc. Tech. (home economics, Ind. Arts, etc.)	2
Elementary Education	8
Other	16

Table 1.38 concludes this section on an encouraging note. Sixty-two percent of leadership team members plan to remain in their present positions for the next three to five years. The career goal of the next largest percentage is the building principalship or assistant principalship. These career plans are in the best interest of the schools. It would appear that the next generation of middle level principals will be even better prepared than the contemporary group to exercise effective leadership.

TABLE 1.38

Leadership Team Member Career Plan for Next 3–5 Years

Career Plans	1992
Remain in Present Position	62
Retirement	3
Seek Position as Bldg. Principal or Assistant Principal	22
Seek Different Teaching Position at the Middle Level	2
Seek Different Teaching Position at Another Grade Level	2
Seek a Position in a Junior College or University	1
Seek a Position in a State Department of Education or Other Educational Service Agency (other than a school district)	1
Undecided	5
Other	1

Summary

The typical middle level principal is a white male between 40 and 50 years of age, with a master's degree, more than 7 years in the principalship, and 10 or more years of teaching experience. He has served as an assistant principal, a department chair or team leader, and has had some coaching experience. He administers a middle school with grades 6-7-8 and plans to remain in his present position for three to five years.

Typical middle level assistant principals and leadership team members are somewhat younger, have been in their positions fewer years than principals, and plan to remain in their present positions for the next three to five years. Dramatic increases have taken place in the numbers of female middle level leaders, constituting in 1992 21 percent of the principals, 35 percent of assistant principals, and 66 percent of leadership team members.

Chapter 2

School Leadership

In the late '70s and early '80s, the role of the principal underwent a modest transformation from school manager to instructional leader. Curriculum development and instructional supervision were commonly accepted as appropriate roles for principals. Perhaps few principals completely realized an active instructional role, but the stage was set for the mid-to-late '80s, when educational restructuring became the pervasive theme in administration.

Bureaucratic decentralization was a primary focus of many restructuring efforts, with site-based management, shared governance, and teacher empowerment the most important collaborative initiatives among administrators, teachers, support staff, parents, and community leaders. Recommended practices included "team leadership," with emphasis on participative strategies, consensus seeking, and conflict resolution. Leadership teams, instructional councils, and advisory committees were pervasive examples of collaboration.

Principals were urged to involve all stakeholders in decisions affecting individuals as well as the entire school organization. Principals worked to develop cultures of trust that would promote and support positive relationships among members of the school community. The decade of the '80s saw changing role expectations for school leaders.

Findings presented in this study describe leadership practices in the middle level schools of 1992, the extent to which those practices changed from 1981 and 1966, and the degree to which 1992 practices conformed to recommended leadership practices. This chapter includes sections on the preparation of leaders, staffing practices, leadership tasks, participative decision making, and job satisfaction.

Preparation for Leadership

Principals in 1992 are older than the principals in the 1981 study; they have more years of teaching and fewer years of administrative experience. Many, if not the majority, of contemporary middle level principals received their formal preparation and began their administrative careers during the constantly changing '80s.

Why did these educators decide to enter administration? Did graduate programs effectively prepare them? What factors influenced their selection as principals? These are among the interesting questions to consider when reviewing the findings in this section.

❑ Making the Leadership Choice

Principals and assistant principals indicated that the factor most important to their decision to enter administration was the opportunity to help students and others by using their creative leadership abilities and aptitudes. Low on the list of factors were salary, recognition, status, prestige, security, working hours, and vacation time.

Many principals, assistant principals, and members of leadership teams were influenced by specific individuals in their decision to enter administration or teaching. For principals and assistant principals, other administrators and colleagues were more influential than professors or family members. For teachers serving on leadership teams, parents and professors had the most influence on their decision to enter the profession.

Assistant principals were asked to identify the point in their careers when they decided to enter administration. Sixty-eight percent said they made the decision after 5 or more years of educational experience. Twenty-five percent decided during the first 4 years of their career, and 7 percent said they decided at about the same time they entered the profession. The majority of assistant principals entered administration with more than 10 years of teaching experience.

❑ Securing the Position

Principals and assistant principals reported those factors that most contributed to their ability to secure their first principalship or assistant principalship. The factors are ranked in Table 2.1 from most to least important. For both groups, key factors included success and years in current position as teacher or assistant principal, amount and quality of professional preparation, success during the job interview, success on formal assignments outside the classroom, contacts within the profession, the superintendent or principal "wanted me," and "being at the right spot at the right time."

Contacts outside the profession were relatively unimportant. The lowest rated responses were options not available equally to all respondents, such as assessment center reports, performance on competitive exams, and service as a librarian or counselor.

Principals and assistant principals were asked to describe the extent to which certain "individuals affected the final decision to appoint you to your current position." As expected, superintendents had the most impact on the decision to appoint a principal. Principals and superintendents

146,890

TABLE 2.1

Ranking of Factors Contributing to First Appointment

PRINCIPAL	ASSISTANT PRINCIPAL
1. Success as a teacher	1. Success as a teacher
2. Successful job interview	2. Performance in formal assignments outside the classroom
3. Success as assistant principal	3. Contacts within the profession
4. Superintendent or assistant superintendent wanted me	4. The principal wanted me
5. Amount/quality of professional preparation	5. Amount/quality of professional preparation
6. Contacts within the profession	6. I was at the right spot at the right time
7. Performance in formal assignments outside the classroom	7. Successful job interview
8. I was at the right spot at the right time	8. Number of years of teaching experience
9. Performance of informal assignments outside the classroom	9. The superintendent or assistant superintendent wanted me
10. Number of years of experience as an assistant principal	10. Performance of informal assignments outside the classroom
11. Number of years of teaching experience	11. Contacts outside the profession
12. Contacts outside the profession	12. Success as a counselor, librarian, etc.
13. Success as a counselor, librarian, etc.	13. Assessment center report
14. Assessment center report	14. Performance on competitive exams
15. Performance on competitive exams	

had the most impact on decisions to appoint assistant principals. Boards of education usually make the final, legal decisions about employment, but neither boards, professors, nor other professional contacts had much impact on the final decisions.

Principals and assistant principals also rated the importance of specific issues in the preparation for their current positions. In Table 2.2, the percentage of principals or assistant principals reporting an issue is listed in the parentheses immediately following the issue; their responses to the degree of influence are listed in the columns.

Eighty percent of the principals have been assistant principals. Eighty-seven percent of those who were assistants said that the experience had "great" influence on their preparation for the principalship. For both principals and assistant principals, work as a teacher was a major contributor to their preparation. Professional experiences, including work as an activity adviser, department head, team leader, and school leadership team member were also perceived as significant contributors. University coursework and field experiences were perceived as less important.

TABLE 2.2

Contribution to Preparation for Current Position

PRINCIPALS	None	Little or Moderate	Great
Work as an assistant principal (80%)	5	8	87
Work as a teacher (99%)	1	26	73
Work as an adviser of a student activity (86%)	7	43	50
Work as a guidance counselor (25%)	36	12	52
Work as a department head or team leader (59%)	9	34	57
Work as a member of school leadership team (67%)	10	39	51
Participation in community activities (96%)	11	51	38
Participation in professional activities (98%)	7	39	54
University coursework (99%)	4	62	34
University field experience (86%)	13	59	29

ASSISTANT PRINCIPALS	None	Little or Moderate	Great
Work as a teacher (99%)	1	15	84
Work as an adviser of a student activity (86%)	7	38	55
Work as a guidance counselor (28%)	37	12	51
Work as a department head or team leader (69%)	8	32	60
Work as a member of school leadership team (68%)	6	29	65
Participation in community activities (93%)	11	51	38
Participation in professional activities (97%)	8	46	46
University coursework (99%)	8	55	37
University field experience (87%)	17	48	35

(Figures in parentheses indicate the percentage of respondents with that experience.)

Principals and assistant principals also described the assistance given to them in their current role. Principals said that other principals and central office staff members most directly influenced their ability to function effectively in their current job. Assistant principals said that principals and other assistant principals most directly influenced their ability to function effectively.

Staffing Practices

In the opening paragraphs of this section, the evolving role of the principalship was briefly discussed. Leadership teams were mentioned as a common participative management strategy. Principals, assistant principals, and members of leadership teams were asked numerous questions in this study about the existence and practices of leadership teams in their middle level schools.

❏ The Leadership Team

Principals were asked to indicate whether the school had a leadership team based on the following definition: *A leadership team is a group of teachers and administrators designated by the principal or elected by the faculty to assist in the leadership operation of the school. These staff members may have been formally designated, or they may be a more informal group obviously instrumental in the ongoing operation of the school.*

Sixty-eight percent of the principals reported leadership teams in their schools. Sixty-one percent of the members of the leadership teams said they were a part of the team in a "formal way through job title and responsibilities." The others indicated that they functioned in a more "informal way, without having a formal job title or responsibility."

Principals, assistant principals, and members of leadership teams all described the make-up of their teams. Teams typically included seven or more persons, both male and female. Teachers, assistant principals, counselors, and team leaders were, in order, the persons most frequently serving on these teams. Others were coordinators, deans, interns, parents, and support staff. It is interesting to speculate why only 54 percent of the principals reported teachers as part of the school leadership team. In contrast, assistant principals and leadership team members said teachers were a part of the team in approximately 75 percent of the schools. This difference of opinion suggests that leadership team membership in many schools is not well defined.

TABLE 2.3

Leadership Team Characteristics

Schools with teams	68
Formality of teams	
Formal membership	61
Informal membership	39
Size of teams	
Three or fewer	7
Four	7
Five	7
Six	10
Seven	13
More than seven	56
Female membership on teams	
Two or fewer	24
Three or four	34
Five or six	20
Seven or more	22
Teacher membership on teams as described by...	
Principals	54
Assistant principals	73
Leadership team members	77

❏ Assistant Principals

In 1992, as in 1981, 77 percent of the principals reported one or more assistant principals in their schools (Table 2.4). Of schools with assistants, 10 percent had one part-time assistant; 58 percent, one full-time assistant; 23 percent, two assistants; and 8 percent, three or more assistants. One percent of the schools did not have a person called an assistant principal, but had someone with an equivalent position. Forty-three percent of the schools reported one or more female assistant principals.

TABLE 2.4

Number of Assistant Principals

Schools with Assistant Principals

1992	77
1981	77
1992 Assistant principals per school	
One—part time	10
One—full time	58
Two	23
Three or more	8
None—but an equivalent position	1
1992 Female assistants	
None	57
One	39
Two	3
Three or more	1

❏ Female Teaching Staff

In 1981, 62 percent of the middle level schools across the United States had teaching staffs composed of half or more females. By 1992, 86 percent of staff members were female. Was this increase a result of the dramatic decrease in junior high schools from 1981 to 1992, and a corresponding increase in middle schools? This shifting pattern may be partially responsible, but also consider the gender distribution by grade level presented in Table 2.5. Not only did each type of grade pattern have an increase in the number of female teachers, but the largest increases were in the 7–8, 7–8–9, and "other" schools. Apparently, all of middle level education has experienced a decline in male staff.

Researchers and practitioners should give special attention to this issue. For many students, middle level schooling is their first significant experience with male teachers. If the shifting pattern continues at the present drastic rate, middle level schools will resemble elementary schools in male/female teacher composition. This will be an abnormal middle level environment for all students, but especially for boys needing male role models during the developmental years.

TABLE 2.5

Percent of Schools with Half or More Female Teachers

	1981	1992
All Schools	62	86
By Grades		
6-7-8	84	89
5-6-7-8	80	83
7-8	58	91
7-8-9	58	82
Other	57	94

❑ Teacher Certification

Middle level teachers primarily hold secondary certification, although the availability of "middle level" teaching certification has increased in recent years. Prior to 1981, 38 percent of the states offered middle school teaching certificates; now 66 percent have middle school certification (Valentine, 1992). From 1981 to 1992, however, certification patterns have not reflected this greater availability. Middle level certification has remained at 11 percent. In fact, there has been a decline in secondary certification among middle level teachers and a proportionate increase in elementary certification. Only 9 percent of the principals in 1981 said that the majority of their teachers had elementary certificates; by 1992, the number had increased to 26 percent. The increase in elementary certification may primarily reflect the increase in schools with grade patterns of 6-7-8, 5-6-7-8, and 7-8, and the decrease in those with 7–8–9 patterns. Yet, elementary certification increased and secondary certification decreased for all grade patterns.

Like the ratio of female to male teachers, this certification trend is important. Unlike the female-male pattern, the trend is viewed by most middle level researchers as positive. For many years, middle level educators have encouraged a useful mix of elementary and secondary teachers to meet the needs of developing adolescents. This elementary certification uptrend is a move in that direction.

Leadership Roles and Responsibilities

Staff and community members interpret the mission of the school by observing what principals and other building-level leaders emphasize, and how they spend their time. School leaders establish and perpetuate the culture of the school by their job tasks. This section details these roles and responsibilities of school leaders, including how they spend their time.

❑ Typical Work Week

Building leaders work many hours each week. This is especially true for principals. Eighty-eight percent of the principals reported working an average of more than 50 hours in a typical week (Table 2.7). Thirty percent reported a typical week of more than 60 hours, and 6 percent, more

TABLE 2.6

Distribution of Teacher Certification

	Elementary	Middle	Secondary
All Schools:			
1981	9	11	80
1992	26	11	63
By Grade Level:			
6–7–8 Schools			
1981	16	21	63
1992	27	13	60
5–6–7–8			
1981	40	10	50
1992	46	11	43
7–8			
1981	10	8	82
1992	15	4	81
7–8–9			
1981	2	7	91
1992	3	10	87

than 70 hours. From 1966 to 1981, the self-reported number of work hours was constant. The number is up significantly since 1981, with twice as many principals reporting 60–69 hours per week, and three times as many reporting 70 or more. Principals are spending significantly more time on the job than in previous years.

Data for assistant principals and team leaders were not available for 1966 or 1981. In 1992, assistant principals reported working fewer hours than principals, with 59 percent reporting work weeks of 50 or more hours. Members of the leadership teams reported somewhat fewer hours, with 51 percent working an average of 50 hours or more.

TABLE 2.7

Principal Self-Reported Hours for Average Work Week

	Principals			Assistants
	1992	1981	1966	1992
40	0	1	4	5
40–49	12	27	27	36
50–59	52	55	54	47
60–69	30	15	12	10
70+	6	2	3	2

❑ Job Descriptions

Nearly all principals (90 percent) and assistant principals (84 percent) had written job descriptions. By contrast, fewer than half (41 percent) the leadership team members had job descriptions for their team roles. Whether or not they had written job descriptions, assistant principals and leadership team members said that the principal was the most significant person identifying the duties and responsibilities for their positions.

For assistant principals, typically the principal and assistant principal worked together or with others to define the assistant's role. However, in 42 percent of the schools, the assistant had virtually no input into the role. In 24 percent of those schools, the principal established the role; in 3 percent, the superintendent did so; and in 15 percent, the principal and superintendent or school board jointly set the role.

The duties and responsibilities of leadership team members were established by the principal and/or assistant principal in concert with the team member 36 percent of the time, by the principal alone 42 percent of the time, and by the principal and assistant 11 percent of the time. Eight percent of the assistant principals and 83 percent of the members of the leadership teams had classroom teaching assignments in addition to their leadership responsibilities. In fact, 64 percent of leadership team members taught more than four courses.

❑ Allocation of Time for a Typical Work Week

Principals and assistant principals were asked to describe both how they *do* spend their time and how they *should* spend their time during a typical work week. The responses of current principals are contrasted with those of principals in 1981, and the rank ordering of the nine responsibility areas is presented in Table 2.8. These rankings are based on the median scores for each area. A rank of 1 indicates the greatest amount of time spent; 9 indicates the least amount of time.

Little change has occurred over the past 12 years in the rank ordering of the time principals spend on specified areas of responsibility and the time they believe they should spend. School management continues to be the area in which principals do spend most of their time. In both 1981 and 1992, principals said that program development was the area where they *should* spend their time. Program development dropped one place in the rank ordering from 1981 to 1992, moving job practice further away from role expectations. The rankings of "do spend" and "should spend" for the areas of personnel, student behavior, and district office remained the same from 1981 to 1992. Planning and professional development moved up in the expectations column, indicating that principals attribute more importance to those areas than in 1981. By way of contrast, time that *should* be spent on student activities and community moved down the priority list.

Ranking how assistant principals reported their time provides a rather traditional picture of life as an assistant. The assistants saw their primary role as working with students on behavior. They rated program development second in priority, but student activities second for time spent. They ranked personnel third in priority, but day-by-day management of the school third for time spent. They, like principals, rated district office meetings, task forces, reports, etc., lowest in priority but higher on the "do spend" list.

Drawing conclusions from self-perceived ratings of time spent must be done cautiously, but two patterns of "real" and "ideal" time spent can be noted. First, principals gave priority to time

School Leadership

FIGURE 2.8

Rank Order of Time Allocation for a Typical Work Week—(1992 Principals)

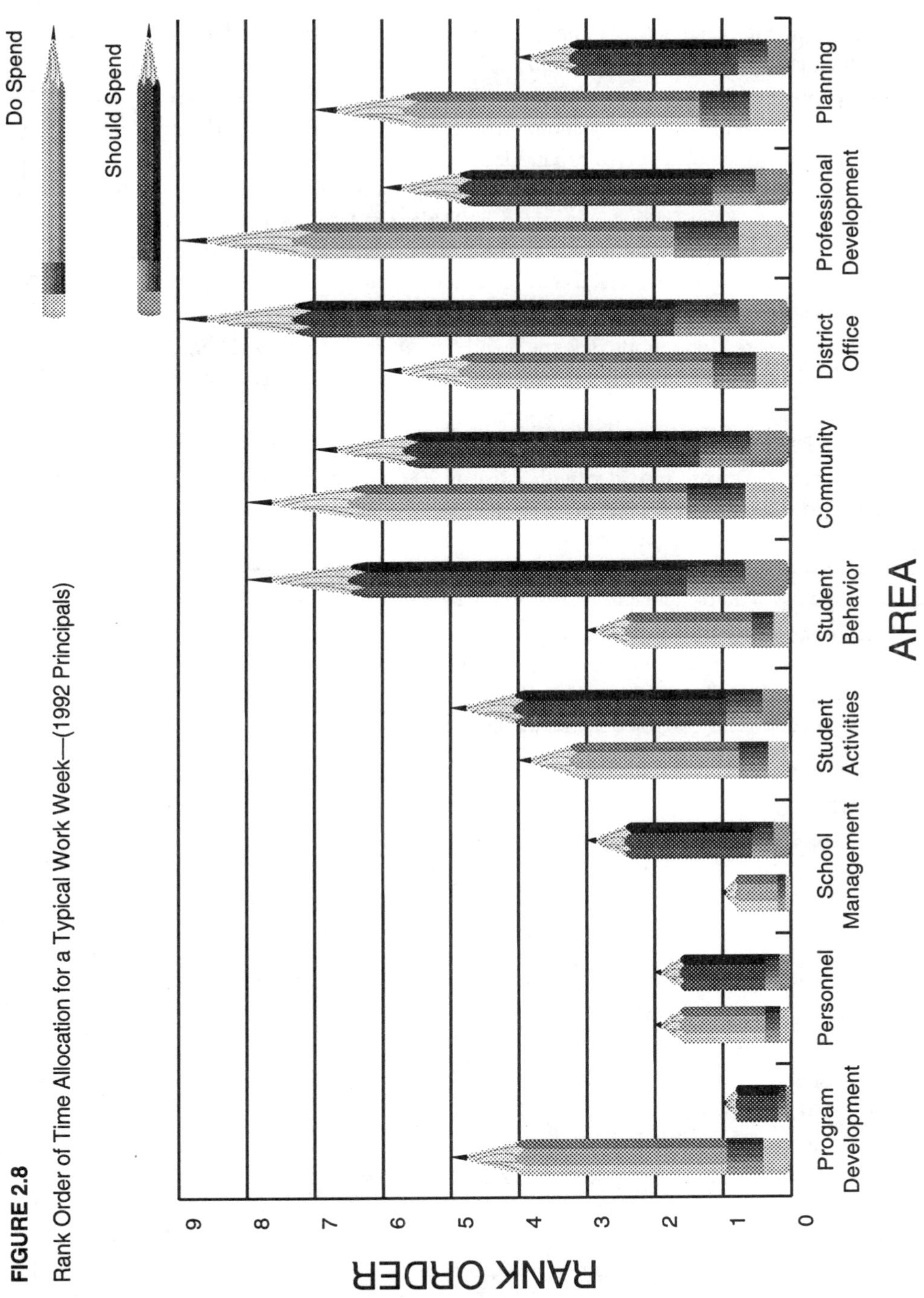

spent on areas of responsibility commonly associated with instructional leadership, such as program development, personnel, planning and professional development, but little real progress has been made in reordering how they actually spend their time.

Only personnel appeared near the top of how principals spent their time in both 1981 and 1992; program development and planning lost ground during those same years. Second, the role of the assistant principal revolves around student discipline, attendance, and activities. To conclude that the assistant principal has not emerged as a partner in the operations of the school goes beyond the scope of the findings presented in Table 2.8 A ranking of seventh for planning and ninth for program development, however, raises the question of how assistants could possibly be viewed, or could view themselves, as critical to the instructional leadership of the school when so little time is spent on these areas.

The following section reports in some detail the *duties and responsibilities of assistant principals and leadership team members* and the decision-making authority given to them.

❑ Duties and Responsibilities

Assistant principals were provided with a list of 20 duties commonly associated with their role and asked to indicate the degree of *responsibility,* the degree of *importance,* and the degree of *discretionary behavior* associated with each duty. Leadership team members were given the same list and asked to respond relative to their roles. Principals were also asked to assess the duties of the assistant principals.

Three options were given for the *degree of responsibility* that an assistant principal or leadership team member might have for each duty: *minor responsibility,* defined as the principal does the job—the assistant/leadership team member provides assistance at the principal's discretion; *moderate responsibility,* defined as the job is delegated but closely supervised by the principal—

TABLE 2.8

Leaders Rank Order of Time Allocation for a Typical Work Week

Area of Responsibility	1992 Principal		1981 Principal		1992 Asst. Prin.	
	Do Spend	Should Spend	Do Spend	Should Spend	Do Spend	Should Spend
School management	1	3	1	3	3	5
Personnel	2	2	2	2	4	3
Student behavior	3	8	3	8	1	1
Student activities	4	5	5	4	2	4
Program development	5	1	4	1	9	2
District office	6	9	6	9	8	9
Planning	7	4	8	5	7	7
Community	8	7	7	6	6	6
Professional development	9	6	9	7	9	8

the principal and assistant/leadership team member work together; and *major responsibility,* defined as the job is delegated and not closely supervised—the assistant/leadership team member is held responsible for the job.

Respondents were also asked to rate the *importance* of a delegated duty to the effective functioning of the school. The three response options were: *minor importance,* defined as the job is not very important—if it is not completed effectively there will not be a significant negative impact on overall school effectiveness; *moderate importance,* defined as the job is important—if it is not completed effectively, the overall effectiveness of the school is diminished; and *major importance,* defined as the job is critical—if it is not completed effectively, the overall effectiveness of the school is significantly impaired.

Finally, respondents were asked to describe the *degree of discretionary behavior* associated with each duty. The three options were: *minor discretionary behavior,* defined as the behavior needed to complete the function is almost completely dictated by others—the assistant/leadership team member makes few, if any decisions; *moderate discretionary behavior,* defined as the behavior needed to complete the function is generally self-directing, with little direction from others—the assistant/leadership team member has the opportunity to make most decisions associated with this duty; and *major importance,* defined as the behavior needed to complete the function is completely self-directing—the assistant/leadership team member receives no direction from others and makes all decisions associated with this duty.

Table 2.9 shows the responses of principals about their assistant principals and the self-perceived responses of assistant principals and leadership team members. The numbers in the table are averages; the higher the number, the more significant the response for that behavior. Analysis provided few surprises. Generally, principals and assistants viewed the duties of assistants in a similar manner. Assistants were responsible for more traditional, managerial tasks rather than instructional leadership functions. The degree of discretionary behavior paralleled the degree of responsibility. Assistants typically viewed their duties as having less discretionary behavior than was reported by their principals. The following paragraphs offer more detailed explanations of the data in Table 2.9.

The duty area for which assistant principals were given the greatest responsibility was "discipline/attendance." This responsibility (2.8 on a 3.0 scale) was ranked significantly higher than any other duty. "Transportation," "community relations," "building use/calendar," "cocurricular activities," and "interscholastic sports" were next in order of responsibility as described by principals. The perceptions of assistant principals were very similar. The notable exception was "community relations"; principals said their assistants had more responsibility than the assistants perceived.

Leadership team members reported duties associated with curriculum and instruction as their primary responsibilities. These included "department teams," "adviser/advisee programs," "instructional materials," "curriculum," "instructional improvement," and "interdisciplinary teams."

Responses from principals, assistant principals, and leadership team members supported the importance of instructional leadership duties for assistant principals and leadership team members. The two exceptions were "discipline and attendance," which was the highest rated item of importance for assistants and third highest for leadership team members, and "community relations," which was high for both groups. The most important instructional leadership duties for both assistants and team members were "scheduling," "curriculum," "instructional improvement," "school goal setting," and "staff development." When the responses of all groups were combined, "interscholastic sports" was least important to the critical functioning of the school.

"Discipline/attendance" was the duty for which assistant principals were given the greatest degree of discretionary behavior. The degree of discretionary behavior typically paralleled the degree of responsibility ascribed to a duty. In other words, a duty with high responsibility had a relatively high degree of discretionary behavior; a duty of low responsibility, a relatively low degree of discretionary behavior. The amount of discretionary behavior ascribed was typically slightly less than the degree of responsibility. "Discipline/attendance" was the sole exception, with a somewhat bigger difference between responsibility and amount of discretionary behavior.

Principals consistently reported more discretionary behavior for assistants than the assistants described. Most of the reputed differences were relatively small; those for community relations were notable.

TABLE 2.9

Duties of Assistant Principals and Leadership Team Members

Duty:	Principals re (Assistants)			Assistants (Self)			Team Members (Self)		
	R	I	D	R	I	D	R	I	D
Adviser/Advisee Programs	1.9	2.2	1.9	1.8	2.2	1.7	2.1	2.1	1.9
Articulation w/ Elem. School	1.7	2.1	1.8	1.7	2.0	1.7	1.8	2.1	1.6
Articulation w/ High School	1.8	2.1	1.8	1.7	2.1	1.7	1.8	2.1	1.7
Building Use/Calendar	2.1	2.2	2.0	2.0	2.2	1.9	1.5	2.0	1.5
Community Relations	2.2	2.4	2.2	1.9	2.5	1.9	1.7	2.3	1.7
Cocurricular Activities	2.1	2.4	2.1	2.1	2.2	2.0	1.9	2.1	1.7
Curriculum	1.8	2.4	1.9	1.8	2.5	1.7	2.0	2.6	1.8
Department Teams	1.9	2.3	2.0	1.9	2.3	1.8	2.2	2.3	1.9
Discipline/Attendance	2.8	2.8	2.6	2.8	2.8	2.5	1.9	2.5	1.8
Guidance/Health Services	1.8	2.2	1.9	1.8	2.3	1.8	1.8	2.3	1.6
Instructional Improvement	2.0	2.5	2.0	2.0	2.5	1.9	2.0	2.5	1.9
Instructional Materials	1.9	2.2	1.8	1.8	2.3	1.7	2.1	2.3	1.9
Interdisciplinary Teams	1.9	2.3	1.9	1.9	2.3	1.7	2.0	2.3	1.9
Interscholastic Athletics	2.1	2.1	2.0	2.0	2.0	1.8	1.7	1.9	1.5
Parental Involvement	1.8	2.1	1.9	1.8	2.1	1.8	1.7	2.0	1.7
Scheduling	2.0	2.5	1.9	2.0	2.6	1.9	1.8	2.6	1.6
School Goal Setting	2.0	2.4	1.9	1.9	2.4	1.8	1.9	2.4	1.8
Staff Development	1.9	2.4	1.9	1.9	2.4	1.8	1.8	2.3	1.7
Support Staff	2.0	2.3	2.0	1.9	2.2	1.8	1.4	2.1	1.4
Transportation	2.2	2.2	2.1	2.0	2.2	1.8	1.3	2.0	1.2

KEY: **R**esponsibility, **I**mportance, **D**iscretionary Behavior

---

Decision-Making Procedures

Scholars have contended for years that shared decision making improves both the quality of decisions and the commitment to decisions once made. In recent research, shared decision making has been associated with improved employee job satisfaction and morale, increased productivity, reduced resistance to change, and reduced absenteeism (Duttweiler, 1990). The data and discussion that follow provide a clear, but somewhat disappointing, picture of participative decision making in typical middle level schools throughout the country.

❏ Participative Decision Making

Principals were asked to indicate whether, and at what level, selected individuals and groups were involved in decisions about different operations of their schools. The data in Table 2.10 represent the percentage of schools in which individuals/groups were involved in the decision-making process. For those involved, the number in the table below the percentage is an average score for the pattern of involvement. The averages were computed in this way: "1" means that the person was involved in the discussions that led to a decision; "2" means the person made recommendations for a decision; and "3" indicates the person made the actual decision. Thus, the higher the percentage and the accompanying score, the greater the degree of involvement.

The first five issues listed in the table are commonly associated with instructional leadership; the remaining ones are staff, fiscal, and student issues. For all issues, principals were most frequently and highly involved in the decision-making process.

The formulation of school goals and mission involved more persons, and involved them at a higher level, than any other issue. Except for students, central office staff, and school board members, all other persons were involved in these decisions in at least 70 percent of the schools. The levels of involvement were at or above 2.0 for each group except individual teachers, students, and parents/community. Central office staff and board members were not involved as frequently as most other groups, but when they were involved, the level of their involvement was high.

Curricular reform also had a broad base of involvement, but the level was lower for all groups except central office and school board. Decisions about grading practices and teams or departments involved persons at the school site more than the other decisions. When central office staff and school board members were involved, their involvement was significant. The pattern of involvement appears to be broad-based for formulation of school goals and school-based for operational issues, with central office and board members highly involved in the final decisions.

Principals, central office staff, and board members were frequently and highly involved in staff employment decisions. Principals and assistant principals were primarily responsible for the evaluation of staff members. Principals, central office staff, and board members were most frequently and highly involved in the development of the school budget.

The development of rules for student behavior had the broadest base of involvement of all issues. Involvement was highest for principals, assistant principals, leadership team members, central office staff, and board members.

Given the contemporary emphasis on need for participative involvement through leadership teams and staff committees, we conducted a more detailed analysis of the involvement of these groups in the decision-making process. Leadership teams were more frequently involved in decisions about instructional and student behavior, less involved in budgetary development, and seldom involved in staff employment or evaluation decisions. Their involvement for all issues was typically in making recommendations, not reaching decisions.

When leadership teams were involved in decisions, principals said that they made the actual decisions about goals and mission in 34 percent of the schools (highest), and about new courses or programs in only 9 percent of the schools (lowest). The most negative finding was the percent

---

TABLE 2.10

Principals' Descriptions of Individuals' Participation in Decision Making

Issue:	PR	AP	LT	TD	SC	FW	IT	ST	PC	CO	SB
Formulating goals/mission **	96	75	70	72	79	91	85	58	76	65	52
*	2.5	2.1	2.2	2.0	2.0	2.0	1.6	1.4	1.5	2.0	2.2
Curricular reform	97	72	69	74	78	82	85	42	71	86	79
	2.3	1.8	1.8	1.8	1.8	1.6	1.5	1.2	1.3	2.3	2.7
New courses or programs	96	70	68	75	74	72	85	39	66	85	80
	2.3	1.6	1.7	1.7	1.7	1.4	1.5	1.2	1.3	2.3	2.7
Evaluating grading practices	96	73	67	70	74	86	79	38	61	73	59
	2.5	2.0	2.0	1.9	1.8	1.7	1.6	1.3	1.3	2.2	2.4
Teams vs. Departments	87	66	59	64	64	72	66	23	44	66	53
	2.6	2.0	2.0	2.0	1.8	1.7	1.4	1.3	1.3	2.3	2.5
Hiring teaching staff	96	69	33	51	30	19	27	4	12	79	73
	2.5	2.0	1.8	1.8	1.8	1.4	1.3	1.4	1.4	2.4	2.8
Evaluating teaching staff	96	75	20	29	10	13	27	6	10	51	25
	2.9	2.5	1.8	1.7	1.4	1.4	1.2	1.2	1.2	2.0	2.4
Developing school budget	89	65	56	64	53	63	65	13	33	77	66
	2.5	1.8	1.8	1.8	1.6	1.5	1.4	1.3	1.4	2.5	2.8
Rules of student behavior	96	78	68	66	75	89	84	73	74	64	68
	2.6	2.2	2.0	1.7	1.7	1.7	1.6	1.3	1.4	2.1	2.6

(PR=Principal; AP=Assistant Principal; LT=Leadership Team; TD=Team Leaders or Department Chairs; SC=Staff Committee; FW=Faculty as a whole; IT=Individual Teacher; ST=Students; PC=Parents or Community; CO=Central Office; SB=School Board)

* Average of responses for pattern of involvement:
   1 = Involved in discussion
   2 = Makes recommendations
   3 = Makes decisions
** Percent involved in decision-making process

of schools where the members of the leadership teams were involved only in the discussions, not in making recommendations or decisions. For example, the leadership team was three times more likely to be involved in the discussion than in making the decision; for new courses/programs, for curriculum reform, budget development, and evaluation of teachers the ratio was approximately two to one for discussion over decision making.

When staff committees were involved in the decision-making process, they typically made recommendations, not decisions. The only exception was staff evaluation, where, in 10 percent of the schools, their role was providing input. Staff committees were most frequently involved in instructional and student behavioral issues. When involved, they made decisions about goals and mission in 22 percent of the schools, about hiring staff in 17 percent, and about teams or departments in 14 percent. They were involved in decisions about new courses/programs and budget development in only 4 percent of the schools, and about teacher evaluation in less than 1 percent.

Generally, the 1992 findings do not reflect a high degree of active involvement in decision making on the part of leadership teams or staff committees. No issues were cited in which either of these two groups were involved in more than 80 percent of the schools. The level of involvement was most typically in making recommendations or only in discussion. Decision making was infrequent.

A comparison of the 1992 data with the questions asked of principals in 1981 provide little evidence that participative management strategies have increased or decreased significantly. In the 1981 survey, principals reported on the frequency of involvement for most of the same issues in the current survey. From 1981 to 1992, nearly twice as many issues declined in stakeholder involvement as increased. Typically, changes were fewer than 5 percentage points.

The most notable patterns of increasing involvement affected assistant principals, individual teachers, and parents/community. The greatest declines in involvement were by department chairs/team leaders and the faculty as a whole.

Because the 1981 study did not ask about leadership teams and staff committees, a true comparison is difficult. It would be plausible if involvement of department chairs/team leaders and the faculty as a whole had been displaced by involvement of leadership team members and staff committees. However, the 1992 findings that indicate infrequent involvement by leadership team members and staff committees would suggest that this was not the case.

The overall picture of participative management by shared decision making is disappointing. The degree of change in the past 12 years and the level of impact of shared decision making in typical middle level schools across the nation is modest at best.

A word of caution is particularly appropriate in interpreting the reported degree of involvement of central office staff and board members. Respondents were specifically asked to respond about involvement in the decision-making process "at the building level." Responses about central office staff and board members may be misleading.

Some principals may have focused on the involvement of central office staff and board members after the decision-making process moved from the building level to the central office and board levels, where those persons are typically involved in making the final decisions. If the responses do accurately reflect central office and board member roles in decision making at the building level, site-based management has made even less impact than was implied in the previous discussion.

❑ Budgeting/Staffing Authority

Principals were asked, "To what extent do you participate in determining the budget allocation for your school?" Respondents had a slightly greater degree of participation in 1992 than in 1981 (Table 2.11). Thirty percent of the principals described their participation as high, up 7 percent from 1981; 18 percent had no involvement, down 4 percent from 1981.

TABLE 2.11

Principal Participation in School Budget Allocation

Extent of Participation	1992	1981
High	30	23
Moderate	25	30
Little	27	25
None	18	22

Principals were also asked to describe their degree of authority in the allocation of discretionary monies available to their schools. Respondents in 1992 appear to have greater flexibility in this arena than in 1981. The increase from 16 to 22 percent for "unrestricted authority" is particularly significant.

TABLE 2.12

Principal Authority in Allocation of Discretionary Funds

Extent of Authority	1992	1981
Some authority with restrictions, such as approval by superiors	67	62
Little authority (1981 only)	–	16
No authority	5	6
Unrestricted authority	27	16

Responses to the question, "How much authority do you have to fill teacher vacancies?" are reported in Table 2.13. A trend toward more authority for principals is evident, with 20 percent in 1966, 33 percent in 1981, and 51 percent in 1992 for the response, "I make the selection and central office endorses it." Evidence is strong that principals now play a more critical role in staff selection. The corresponding decline from 19 percent to 2 percent for central office authority further supports this trend.

Principals were also asked to indicate how much authority they had to make alternative personnel decisions, such as employing two or three teacher aides instead of one teacher. Responses

TABLE 2.13

Principal Authority To Fill Teacher Vacancies

Extent of Authority	1992	1981	1966
I make the selection and the central office endorses it.	51	33	20
I make the selection within limited options stipulated by the central office.	23	32	60
I recommend a person to fill the vacancy and the central office makes the decision.	24	26	
The central office selects the teacher to fill the vacancy.	2	9	19
Other	*	*	1

* Data not collected

for 1992 and 1981 are presented in Table 2.14. Although principals do have more general authority in staffing decisions than in previous years, they appear to be losing authority for alternative staffing. Note especially the significant increase in percentage of principals who have "no authority" to make these building-level staffing decisions. Even if the 20 percent in 1981 who had "little authority" were added to the "no authority" category, the decrease would still be significant. Principals do not have the same staffing of flexibility today as they did in 1981.

TABLE 2.14

Principal Authority To Make Alternative Staffing Decisions

Extent of Authority	1992	1981
Unrestricted authority	3	5
Authority with some restrictions, such as approval by superiors	52	62
Little authority	*	20
No authority	45	13

* Data not collected

❑ Parent/Citizen Involvement

Principals were asked two questions about the involvement of parents and members of the community in the operations of their schools. The responses identified the areas in which parents and other citizens were involved in *a planning or advisory capacity*. The number of schools with no parental/citizen involvement for any of the response options dropped from 8 percent in 1981 to 1 percent in 1992.

However, except for "evaluation of programs," the percentages for the other response options common to both the 1981 and 1992 surveys declined. Parents and citizens are more involved in planning and advisory roles in schools, but this involvement is dispersed across more areas. A possible reason for the overall increase may be the high level of involvement in fiscal matters, an option not provided in the 1981 survey.

TABLE 2.15

Parent/Citizen Involvement in Planning or Advisory Capacity

Involvement	1992	1981
Objectives and priorities for the school	49	59
Program changes and new programs being considered	42	59
Student activities	51	67
Student behavior, rights, and responsibilities	32	56
Finance and fund raising	43	*
Evaluation of programs	31	31
Parents or other citizens are not involved in any of the above	1	8

* Data not collected

Principals were asked about those areas in which parents and citizens were involved in the actual operation of the school (Table 2.16). Little change in involvement has occurred since 1981. The most common areas of involvement were in student activity programs, and assisting with instructional programs, including work as aides and tutors. The only noticeable decline (from 66 to 46 percent) was as "resource persons to programs and activities, including instruction."

TABLE 2.16

Parent/Citizen Involvement in School Operation

Involvement	1992	1981
Advisers, counselors to individual students	14	15
Monitors, supervises, sell tickets, etc., for student activities	44	42
Operates concessions, etc., for benefit of school	37	34
Resource persons to programs and activities, including instruction	46	66
Sponsors/moderates student groups	19	23
Volunteer aide	50	48
Volunteer tutor	37	27

Job Satisfaction

The typical middle level principal of 1981 felt that his or her job was self-fulfilling, prestigious, and secure. In 1992, principals, assistant principals, and members of leadership teams were asked to describe their job satisfaction on 11 issues. The issues and average responses for principals, assistant principals, and leadership team members are presented in Table 2.17. The item with the greatest degree of self-perceived job satisfaction for all three respondent groups was rapport with students, followed closely by rapport with teachers. The amount of assistance received from immediate supervisors and the rapport with immediate supervisors were high for assistant principals and leadership team members, but noticeably lower for principals.

On the other hand, principals reported better realization of the expectations they had when they took their jobs than assistant principals and team members. All groups were least satisfied with the amount of time they devoted to the job and with their salaries. For most issues, a majority of respondents selected the option "very satisfied." One-fourth of the assistants and more than one-third of the team members described themselves as "dissatisfied" with salary, but the overall mood of the respondents could only be described as positive. Middle level leaders appear to be well satisfied with the majority of basic job issues.

TABLE 2.17

Degree of Job Satisfaction for Principals, Assistant Principals, and Leadership Teams Members

Degree of Satisfaction	Principals	Assistant Principals	Team Members
The realization of expectations you had when you took the job	2.6	2.4	2.4
The amount of time you devote to the job	2.1	2.1	2.1
The results that you achieve	2.5	2.3	2.8
The salary you receive	2.1	2.0	1.8
The working conditions	2.4	2.4	2.2
The amount of assistance you receive from your immediate supervisor	2.2	2.7	2.6
The rapport you have with your supervisor	2.4	2.8	2.7
The rapport you have with your administrative colleagues	2.7	2.6	2.6
The rapport you have with teachers	2.7	2.6	2.7
The rapport you have with students	2.8	2.7	2.7
The rapport you have with parents and members of the community	2.6	2.6	2.4

Principals, assistants, and team members were also asked how much prestige their positions *provided* and how much they *should provide* (Table 2.18). Principals in 1981 and 1992 believed that their positions provided more prestige than did principals in 1966. Current assistant principals perceived that their jobs had less actual prestige than did principals. Leadership team members ascribed even less prestige to their positions. More than 75 percent of the principals and assistants believe their jobs merited more prestige.

TABLE 2.18

Actual and Ideal Prestige of Principals, Assistants, and Leadership Team Members

	1992 Prin.	1992 Asst. Prin.	1992 Ldshp. Team	1981 Prin.	1966 Prin.
Actual Prestige					
1 Little	< 1	4	12	1	3
2	5	8	21	4	13
3 Moderate	33	33	38	40	50
4	44	42	22	42	30
5 Much	18	13	7	13	4
Ideal Prestige					
1 Little	< 1	1	6	0	–
2	1	< 1	10	1	–
3 Moderate	16	24	38	18	–
4	47	51	36	58	–
5 Much	36	24	10	23	–

In our mobile society, professional educators are frequently faced with the decision to change or not change school districts. Principals, assistant principals, and leadership team members were asked what reasons influenced their decisions about changing districts. The numbers presented in Table 2.19 are average scores. The school environment and a commitment to middle level were the major influences affecting principals' decisions to change or not change districts.

Family commitment and school environment were the major influences for assistant principals; commitment to the middle level and the school environment were the major influences for leadership team members. Job security and family commitment were most frequently described by principals and assistants as having little or no influence on position changes. For leadership team members, family commitment and locale had little or no influence.

To obtain an overall perspective on job satisfaction, each group was asked the general question: "If you could choose again, would you select educational administration as a career?" The responses in Table 2.20 reveal that principals in 1992 were more likely to choose educational administration again than were principals in 1981 or 1966. Views of assistants and team leaders paralleled those of principals. Apparently, most educational leaders are reasonably satisfied with their positions and would again choose educational leadership as a career.

TABLE 2.19

Influences on Decisions To Change or Not Change School Districts

Reasons:	Principals	Assistant Principals	Leadership Team Members
Family commitment motivated me to pass up or not seek other opportunities.	2.1	2.2	2.0
Desire to live in a certain part of the country made me more place than career oriented.	2.2	2.1	2.0
The school environment (e.g., student discipline, parental views) has always been important in my selection of jobs.	2.4	2.2	2.2
Commitment to middle level has caused me to remain at this level rather than change.	2.4	2.1	2.4
Job security, seniority, and retirement benefits outweigh advantages of job changes.	2.0	2.0	2.1

TABLE 2.20

Would You Choose Educational Administration Again?

	1992 Prin.	1992 Asst. Prin.	1992 Ldshp. Team	1981 Prin.	1966 Prin.
Definitely Yes	50	48	56	41	} 64
Probably Yes	31	26	27	27	
Uncertain	10	13	9	15	24
Probably Not	7	11	7	14	} 12
Definitely Not	–	–	–	3	

Summary

This chapter began with a discussion of the evolving role of the principalship, emphasizing the importance of instructional leadership and shared governance. The findings have provided interesting, albeit not always pleasing, insight about these issues.

Principals and assistant principals entered administration so they could use their creative leadership abilities and aptitudes to assist students and teachers. Principals and assistant principals were most directly influenced by administrators and colleagues in their decision to enter administration. Superintendents had the most direct impact on the appointment of principals; principals and superintendents had the most impact on appointment decisions for assistant principals.

Work as a teacher and/or assistant principal and involvement in non-teaching duties such as department head/team leader, leadership team member, and student activity adviser made the greatest contribution to preparation for administration. University coursework and related field experiences received relatively low ratings as contributors.

Principals reported that other principals and central office staff most directly influenced their abilities to function effectively in their current role. Assistant principals said that principals and other assistant principals most directly influenced their ability to function effectively.

> Principals were most directly involved in the decision-making process for all types of building-level decisions. Decisions about school goals and mission involved more persons, and at a higher level, than any other issue.

Leadership teams were present in 68 percent of the schools. Sixty-one percent of these were formal in membership; 39 percent, more informal. Membership on leadership teams typically included seven or more persons, both male and female. Teachers, assistant principals, counselors, and team leaders were, in order, the persons most frequently serving on teams. Principals, assistant principals, and leadership team members disagreed about the makeup of teams, lending support to the conclusion that many teams were actually very informal.

In 1992, as in 1981, 77 percent of the principals had one or more assistant principals. Most had one full-time assistant. Forty-three percent of the schools had one or more female assistant principals.

The percentage of schools with predominantly female teachers increased dramatically since 1981, with the greatest increases in 7–8, 7–8–9, and "other" grade pattern schools. All middle level grade configurations experienced a decline in male staff members. Respondents also reported fewer secondary certificated teachers and a proportionate increase in elementary certificated teachers.

From 1966 to 1981, the number of work hours reported by principals was constant. In this study, twice as many principals reported 60–69 hours per week, and three times as many reported

70 or more hours per week. Little change has occurred during the past decade in the rank ordering of time principals spend on specified areas of responsibility and the time they believe they should spend. School management continues to occupy most of their time, while program development is where they would like to spend their time.

Assistant principal rankings of areas of responsibility provided a rather traditional picture of life as an assistant. The assistants saw their role as working with students on behavior, and they spent their time in that role. They rated program development as second in priority, but student activities as second for time spent. Assistant principals do not appear to be active agents in the instructional operation of the school.

An analysis of the "responsibility," "importance," and "discretionary behavior" for the duties of assistant principals provided few surprises. Generally, principals and assistants viewed the duties in a similar manner. Assistants were responsible for more traditional, managerial tasks rather than instructional leadership functions, with the degree of discretionary behavior paralleling the degree of responsibility.

Principals were most directly involved in the decision-making process for all types of building-level decisions. Decisions about school goals and mission involved more persons, and at a higher level, than any other issue. The 1992 findings do not reveal a high degree of active involvement in decision making on the part of leadership teams or staff committees. The level of involvement was typically in making recommendations or in the discussion of issues. These findings are disappointing. The degree of change in shared decision making during the past 12 years was minimal.

Site-based management assumes high involvement in decisions at the school level. Principals reported more current involvement than in previous years for budget allocation, dispersal of monies, and selection of new staff. However, they had less flexibility to make alternative staffing decisions than in 1981.

Parents and citizens were more involved in planning and advisory roles in 1992 than 1981, but this involvement was dispersed across more issues.

Educational leaders of middle level schools in 1992 were more satisfied with their professional job positions and with the degree of related prestige than respondents were in 1981 or 1966. Although less than satisfied with the number of hours they have to work or the compensation they receive for that work, they value their working relationships with colleagues, students, and parents. They are influenced to remain in their current positions by commitment to middle level education and the school environment in which they work. They are generally satisfied with their jobs and would select middle level administration again if given the opportunity.

Chapter 3

Educational Programs

The call for school reform is pervasive. The president, governors, and U.S. Department of Education have proposed six National Education Goals. One of the goals proposes that students leaving grades 4, 8, and 12 have demonstrated competency in challenging subject matter; another that American students become first internationally in science and mathematics. The question facing middle level educators is, what is their role in this potential revolution?

Middle level education appears to be well positioned for educational transformation. Programs commonly associated with the middle school movement, such as interdisciplinary teaming, block scheduling, and teacher advisory, are examples of restructuring efforts already underway and increasingly advocated even for high schools. Middle level efforts go far beyond typical school improvement at other levels. They focus attention on the way the school is structured, the climate in which teachers work, the way content is organized, and the best environments for learning to take place.

The present study, like the 1981 NASSP study, investigated middle level programs and established comparisons with related research findings. Since the 1981 study, numerous other state and national surveys have produced valuable data. Whenever appropriate, data in this chapter have been related to these other national studies. The two most significant are listed below.

- Alexander et al. (1968)—Surveyed 110 schools having at least three grades, but not more than five, and including grades 7–8; (1989)—Reported on 670 surveys of schools fitting the 1968 criteria plus grade 7–8 and 7–9 schools

- Epstein and Mac Iver (1990)—Sample of 2,400 public schools with grade 7 (1,753 total responses).

Other publications have been cited from the current literature on middle level schooling. These publications include: *Turning Points: Preparing American Youth for the 21st Century* (Carnegie Council on Adolescent Development, 1989); *This We*

Believe (National Middle School Association, 1992); *Agenda for Excellence* (NASSP Council on Middle Level Education, 1985), and related articles in *Phi Delta Kappan's* recent feature issue (1990, Vol. 71 No. 6) on middle level education.

This chapter groups the results of the 1992 NASSP survey according to the following middle level issues: interdisciplinary teaming, grouping of students, instruction, curriculum, cocurricular activities, and interscholastic sports.

Interdisciplinary Teaming

Interdisciplinary team organization has become "a signature practice" in middle level education. This organizational arrangement consists of a team of two to five teachers from different subject areas that assumes responsibility for a group of students, shares a common planning time, and (usually) a location in the same area of the school. Prominent middle level educators believe that interdisciplinary team organization benefits both teachers and students by contributing to a positive school climate. When true interdisciplinary teaming occurs, advocates believe the following results are possible:

1. Teachers experience real collaboration within the work place and become more satisfied professionally.
2. Students feel less isolation, and therefore, more social bonding with peers and individual teachers.
3. Teachers and students develop a strong sense of community and share a common rationale and mission for education.
4. The instructional program becomes highly coordinated across content areas in a way that encourages student creativity and critical thinking.

The Carnegie Council on Adolescent Development (1989) advocated small "communities for learning." One recommendation for achieving this aim was forming teams of teachers and students that would work together to achieve personal as well as academic goals. *This We Believe* (National Middle School Association, 1992) advocated "a range of organizational arrangements" to meet the variety of young adolescent needs. This recommendation envisions the use of interdisciplinary teams with large blocks of time for scheduling student learning activities.

In the current survey, more than half the schools reported some form of interdisciplinary team organization. In 1981, interdisciplinary teaming was used rather infrequently, with departmentalized instruction the predominant practice for grades 6, 7, 8, and 9, and the self-contained classroom the most common practice for grade 5. After a decade of teachers working with students organized into teams, this "signature practice" has increased steadily and research is beginning to proliferate. The National Middle School Association published its first theme issue of *Research in Middle Level Education* on teaming (Arhar, 1992). Universities with strong middle level preparation programs have established research agendas on teaming.

❑ Incidence of Teaming

Principals were asked if their schools had one or more teachers working with an expanded group of students. Teaming schools were asked to respond to survey items that would reveal the characteristics of teaming in their schools. These characteristics included organizing teams, team leaders, team planning, location of team classrooms, team grouping practices, and subject areas teamed.

Results of this survey indicated that 57 percent of the schools surveyed used interdisciplinary teams, an increase of 15 percent over the 1990 survey conducted by Epstein and Mac Iver. Epstein and Mac Iver reported that 7–12, 6–12, and 7–8–9 grade schools did not implement teaming as much as those with 6–7–8 and 5–6–7–8 grade configurations. Alexander and McEwin had concluded in 1989 that almost 33 percent of the schools they surveyed used teaming. The increase in teaming documented by this study has been steady and obvious in recent years. Teaming is becoming the norm, rather than the exception, in middle level schools.

TABLE 3.1

Interdisciplinary Teaming in National Studies

	NASSP 1992	Epstein & Mac Iver 1990	Alexander & McEwin 1989
Have Interdisciplinary Teaming	57	42	33
No Interdisciplinary Teaming	43	58	67

Consistent with previous studies (Table 3.2), the current data showed that middle level schools with grades 6–7–8 use interdisciplinary teaming most often (66 percent), followed by 5–6–7–8 schools. Grade 7–8–9 schools use interdisciplinary teaming the least. Like Epstein and Mac Iver (1990), this survey showed more teaming in the lower grades (Table 3.3). Teaming was almost nonexistent in the ninth grade.

TABLE 3.2

Interdisciplinary Teams by Grade Level Organization

	6–7–8	5–6–7–8	7–8	7–8–9	Other
Have Interdisciplinary Teaming	66	56	44	40	56
No Interdisciplinary Teaming	34	44	56	60	44

❑ Organizing Teams

Teacher certification and endorsements of teachers often predispose team membership, but teacher preference can also be an important consideration in organizing interdisciplinary teams. Principals

TABLE 3.3

Schools with Interdisciplinary Teams by Grade

	5	6	7	8	9
Teaming	49	55	46	38	9
No Teaming	51	45	54	62	91

were asked to indicate how teams of teachers were organized and how team membership was determined. In most middle level schools, teacher teams were organized at the discretion of school administrators with or without teacher input. Of the schools with interdisciplinary team organization, 24 percent reported that administrators alone appointed teachers to specific teams. Sixty-one percent of schools cited teacher input before making decisions about team membership. Only 10 percent of the principals reported that teachers selected their own teams.

Epstein and Mac Iver (1990) asked a similar question of schools that used interdisciplinary teaming in grades 7 or 8 and found that most had administratively arranged teams. They also found that on self-selected teams, teachers spent more time in planning and coordinating instruction and activities.

❏ Team Leaders

Effective team leadership seems to be a significant factor in team success (Erb and Doda, 1989; Merenbloom, 1991). Team leaders facilitate teamwork and serve as liaisons to other school groups and to administrators. Principals were asked about selection, responsibilities, and compensation of team leaders. Of the schools that indicated they used teaming, 77 percent designated a team leader.

TABLE 3.4

Interdisciplinary Team Leaders by Grade Level Organization

	Total	7–8–9	7–8	6–7–8	5–6–7–8	Other
Schools with team leaders	77	75	70	78	79	80
Schools with no team leader	23	25	30	22	21	20

Thirty-seven percent of the principals reported that team leaders were appointed by the administration; 40 percent, that leaders were selected by team membership; and 32 percent, that leadership was rotated among members of the team (Table 3.5). Team leadership seems to be elected or rotated more frequently in 5–6–7–8 schools than in other grade configurations.

TABLE 3.5

Selection of Team Leaders

	Total	7–8–9	7–8	6–7–8	5–6–7–8	Other
Appointed by administration	37	44	48	36	26	40
Selected by team members	40	38	35	39	58	30
Rotated among team members	18	13	17	18	26	10

Ten percent of team leaders were given released time for leadership responsibilities, and 27 percent were given monetary compensation. Schools with grade 6 paid for leadership responsibilities more frequently (Table 3.6).

TABLE 3.6

Compensation of Team Leaders

	Total	7–8–9	7–8	6–7–8	5–6–7–8	Other
Given released time for leader responsibilities	10	13	17	10	0	10
Given monetary compensation for leader responsibilities	27	25	26	28	32	10

❑ Team Planning

Common planning time is critical to the success of interdisciplinary teaming. Common planning offers teachers the opportunity to coordinate instructional content, plan special activities, schedule events, group students for special needs, and arrange conferences with parents.

Principals were asked to choose among statements that described types of team planning. Table 3.7 shows that, of the 57 percent of schools that use teaming, more than one-third have one planning period at the same time for all members of the team. Fifty-four percent said that teams of teachers had one common plus one individual planning period. Fifteen percent reported a planning period, but not necessarily at the same time for all members of the team.

Epstein and Mac Iver (1990) found that almost 30 percent of the schools using interdisciplinary teaming offered no common planning time. They also reported that, in 6–7–8 and 7–8 schools where the majority of the students experience teaming, 36 percent gave teachers two or more hours of common planning time each week.

TABLE 3.7

Teacher Planning Time by Grade Level Organization

	Total	7–8–9	7–8	6–7–8	5–6–7–8	Other
One planning period not necessarily at same time for all team members	15	25	9	17	0	30
One planning period at the same time for all team members	35	44	43	35	26	20
One common planning period for all team members plus an individual planning period	54	25	48	56	79	40

❏ Classroom Location

Proximity of team members' classrooms can facilitate coordination of instruction, allow more flexibility in scheduling, and promote productive collaboration between colleagues. Classrooms scattered about the school are less likely to facilitate a cohesive learning environment.

Principals were asked about the location of classrooms used by teachers on the same team. Table 3.8 shows that 52 percent of the schools using interdisciplinary teams locate the classrooms of *most* teachers on the same team together, with 34 percent reporting *all* classrooms of teachers on the same team adjacent.

TABLE 3.8

Location of Team Classrooms by Grade Level Organization

	Total	7–8–9	7–8	6–7–8	5–6–7–8	Other
Classrooms of all teachers on same team are adjacent	34	27	26	33	47	50
Classrooms of most teachers on same team are adjacent	52	67	56	50	48	40
Classrooms of most teachers on same team are not adjacent	14	6	18	17	5	10

Educational Programs

❑ Number of Students

The survey included questions about the number of students receiving instruction from interdisciplinary teams, the assignment of students to teams, and the subject areas that team members teach. Findings from this study corroborate the previous research of Epstein and Mac Iver (1990) that schools with grade configurations of 6–7–8, 5–6–7–8, and 7–8 use interdisciplinary teaming more than other grade configurations.

Principals were asked to estimate the percentage of their students (excluding special education students) that received instruction from an interdisciplinary team (Table 3.9). Except for 7–8–9 schools, all principals reported that more than half their students received instruction from interdisciplinary teams of teachers.

TABLE 3.9
Percent of Students Receiving Team Instruction by Grade Level Organization

	Total	7–8–9	7–8	6–7–8	5–6–7–8	Other
25 percent or less	6	20	0	6	0	20
26–50 percent	18	33	13	18	11	30
51–75 percent	12	27	9	14	0	0
76–100 percent	64	20	78	63	89	50

In typical teams, students are taught only by the team teachers for the teaming subjects. Seventy-nine percent of the schools reported this practice (Table 3.10). Intact teams of teachers were most often found in schools with grades 7–8, 6–7–8, and 5–6–7–8.

TABLE 3.10
Staffing of Team Instruction by Grade Level Organization

	Total	7–8–9	7–8	6–7–8	5–6–7–8	Other
Students taught only by teachers of their team for "teaming" subject	79	53	87	82	84	56
Students may be taught by non–team teacher for "teaming" subject	21	47	13	18	16	44

❑ Student Assignment to Teams

The organization of the middle school allows for a variety of grouping practices to support various instructional strategies and methodologies. Most middle level scholars seem to concur that heterogeneous grouping of students facilitates higher student achievement and improved sociability, and enhances student self-esteem. (For reviews of this literature, see George, 1988; Oakes, 1985; Spear, 1992.)

Interdisciplinary teaming permits wide flexibility in grouping—for one subject, two subjects, or for mixed groups of students within a classroom. Grouping practices often are decided by the team members for any given group of students. Principals were asked if students were assigned to teams heterogeneously or homogeneously (Table 3.11). Respondents reported much more heterogeneous assignment (88 percent) than homogeneous (12 percent).

TABLE 3.11

Student Team Assignment by Grade Level Organization

	Total	7–8–9	7–8	6–7–8	5–6–7–8	Other
Heterogeneously	88	93	76	90	95	80
Homogeneously	12	7	24	10	5	20

❏ Teaming by Subject Areas

Principals were asked to indicate what subject areas were incorporated into teams (Table 3.12). In middle schools that employed interdisciplinary team organization, math, science, social studies, English/language arts, and reading were the primary subjects involved in teaming. Reading was an exception in 7–8–9 schools, where it seldom was a teaming subject. Some schools have a separate reading course (whole year, semester, or "on the wheel"); some emphasize reading through content areas; still others offer instruction only to remedial students.

TABLE 3.12

Team Subject Areas by Grade Level Organization

	Total	7–8–9	7–8	6–7–8	5–6–7–8	Other
Math, Science, Social Science, English/ Language Arts	34	50	30	33	33	33
Math, Science, Social Science, English/ Language Arts, Reading	51	7	39	59	56	45
Other	15	43	30	8	11	22

Epstein and Mac Iver (1990) found that social studies was taught by at least one team member in 92 percent of the schools that used teaming, followed by English in 91 percent, math in 83 percent, science in 80 percent, and reading in 65 percent. Alexander and McEwin's (1989) survey found that reading was added at the lower grades as a fifth teamed subject. Findings of the current study indicate that team-taught reading has gained prominence in most grade level organizations.

Results of this study, together with the results of other national surveys of middle level programs, indicate that interdisciplinary teaming has definitely increased. The use of *common* and *individual* planning periods has also increased in recent years. Of the schools with teaming, supporting team leadership and common planning time seem more prevalent in 6–7–8 schools. Generally, students are assigned to teams heterogeneously, and the subjects most commonly taught by teams are math, science, social studies, language arts, and reading.

Grouping Students for Instruction

Middle level schools practice a wide variety of grouping strategies. Tracking, ability grouping, homogeneous grouping, and heterogeneous grouping are organizational patterns that traditionally have been thought to be conducive to student learning. Middle level educators are currently considering more flexible ways to group students. Interdisciplinary teaming, peer teaching, cooperative learning, individualized instruction, and multi-age grouping are slowly replacing grouping practices that result in the rigid tracking of students.

Prior achievement, scores on intelligence or achievement tests, and guidance counselor or teacher recommendations have been the factors considered most often when grouping students. Learning styles, student interest, and individual needs are now being utilized. Learning style diagnosis, for example, is used to create ad hoc student groups for cognitive skills training or to honor learning environment preferences (Keefe, 1987).

❏ Ability Grouping

Turning Points: Preparing American Youth for the 21st Century (Carnegie, 1989) asserted that grouping students in classes based on achievement level was almost universal in middle grades schools. *Turning Points,* and an overwhelming abundance of other sources of middle grades education literature, opposed the rigid tracking of students because of its discriminatory and damaging effects on students.

Epstein and Mac Iver (1990) found that more than 40 percent of all middle grades schools utilized between-class ability grouping, and more than 20 percent assigned students to all their classes according to ability. Braddock (1990) similarly reported that two-thirds or more of schools serving young adolescents used some between-class ability grouping, and more than 20 percent assigned students to all classes based on ability.

The 1981 NASSP study examined the extent to which ability grouping was used in middle level schools, the criteria employed for grouping, and the scope of policies for such grouping. The study found that 88 percent of schools grouped students by ability.

In the current study, principals were asked whether their schools did or did not use ability grouping, and if they did, were students grouped into specific classes, or by teachers within classes.

Ability grouping in this study was defined as *the assignment of students to classes based upon academic ability.* Eighty-two percent of the principals said their schools used some degree of ability grouping.

The current study did not measure the entire range of ability grouping practices, but principals did report that almost 70 percent of the schools still grouped students into specific classes by academic ability (Table 3.13). Thirteen percent reported that students were not grouped into specific classes by academic ability, but teachers did group them within their classes.

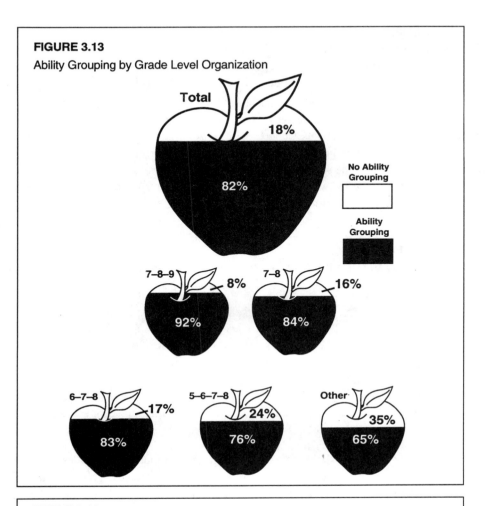

FIGURE 3.13

Ability Grouping by Grade Level Organization

Total

18%

82%

No Ability
Grouping

Ability
Grouping

7–8–9 8%

92%

7–8 16%

84%

6–7–8 17%

83%

5–6–7–8 24%

76%

Other 35%

65%

TABLE 3.13

Ability Grouping by Grade Level Organization

	Total	7–8–9	7–8	6–7–8	5–6–7–8	Other
No form of grouping by academic ability	18	8	16	17	24	35
Students grouped into specific classes by academic ability	69	82	74	68	58	53
Students not grouped into specific classes by academic ability but teachers group within classes	13	10	10	15	18	12

Schools with grades 7–8–9 and 7–8 more often grouped students by academic ability (82 percent and 74 percent respectively) than 6–7–8 and 5–6–7–8 schools (68 percent and 58 percent respectively). However, principals reported that teachers in 6–7–8 and 5–6–7–8 schools grouped students within classes more often than in other grade level organizations.

Table 3.14, comparing the 1981 and 1992 NASSP studies for ability grouping by grade level organization, reveals a slight decrease in the practice across all grade level organizations, with the exception of 7–8–9 schools. Schools with 6–7–8 grades reported a greater decrease in ability grouping than other grade patterns. We did not determine whether students were grouped for all subjects, some subjects, with the same classmates for most subjects, or with the same students for just one or two subjects. Nevertheless, the results of this study indicated a general but small decrease in ability grouping.

TABLE 3.14

Comparison of 1992 and 1981 Studies—Ability Grouping by Grade Level Organization

	Total		6–7–8		5–6–7–8		7–8		7–8–9		Other	
	'92	'81	'92	'81	'92	'81	'92	'81	'92	'81	'92	'81
No Ability Grouping	18	12	17	11	24	20	16	14	8	11	35	18
Ability Grouping	82	88	83	89	76	80	84	86	92	89	65	82

Schools that contained the sixth grade tended to group by academic ability less than schools without grade six. Consistent with the results of the 1981 NASSP study, grouping into specific classes by academic ability remained most common in 7–8–9 schools and least common in 5–6–7–8 schools.

Many educational leaders today are talking about the elimination of ability grouping. Principals were asked to select an appropriate description for the future of ability grouping in their schools (exclusive of practices in special education). Table 3.15 reflects respondents' views on this important issue.

Twenty-nine percent of the schools do not group by ability. Twenty-seven percent reported they have ability grouping and did not plan to change to other grouping practices. Thirty-six percent indicated their students were currently ability grouped, but that they were considering eliminating the practice. Seven percent said they would discontinue ability grouping within the year. Only 1 percent were considering the addition of ability grouping.

Principals of schools with grades 5–6–7–8 more often reported that they do not ability grouping at present and do not plan a change. Almost half the 7–8 schools indicated that they have ability grouping but may eliminate it.

TABLE 3.15

Future of Ability Grouping by Grade Level Organization

	Total	7–9	7–8	6–8	5–8	Other
Have ability grouping and no plans to change	27	34	24	27	26	36
Have ability grouping but may eliminate it	36	39	47	36	23	23
Will eliminate ability grouping within the year	7	11	2	7	6	0
Do not ability group and will continue that way	29	13	27	29	45	41
Do not ability group but considering a change to ability group	1	3	0	1	0	0
Do not ability group but will begin grouping within the next year	0	0	0	0	0	0

❏ Programs for Gifted Students

Gifted student programs—a specialized form of ability grouping—have grown in popularity over the years. Principals were asked to specify the organizational formats for gifted or talented programs in their schools (Table 3.16). Individual projects within regular classes was the predominant method for accommodating gifted students in all grade configurations except 5–6–7–8. These 5–6–7–8 schools provide released time for special classes more often than other grade configurations.

TABLE 3.16

Organizational Format for Gifted Programs by Grade Level Organization

	Total	7–8–9	7–8	6–7–8	5–6–7–8	Other
No gifted program	16	20	15	13	24	11
Released time for special classes	35	23	33	37	44	33
Regular class with individualized projects	51	50	60	52	32	61
After school, evening, or weekend programs	16	20	23	13	24	11
Summer programs	9	10	13	7	12	11
Co–op program with other school	6	10	12	3	9	6
Other	5	10	0	5	3	0

Data in Table 3.17 compare current gifted programs with those reported in 1981. Fourteen percent more middle level schools now offer programs for their gifted or talented students than in 1981. Regular classes with individual projects and released time for special classes remain the most common organizational formats for these programs.

TABLE 3.17

Gifted Program Comparison, 1992 and 1981

	1992	1981
No gifted program	16	30
Have gifted program	84	70
Released time for special classes	35	38
Regular class with individualized projects	51	51
After school, evening, or weekend programs	16	13
Summer programs	9	9
Other	11	31

Principals were also given the opportunity to write in other strategies they used for organizing gifted or talented programs. One principal said that a magnet school had been created for the gifted. Teachers in the magnet were certified in gifted and talented education. Another noted a "Challenge Program" for all students.

Recent research clearly demonstrates that rigid tracking of students is inappropriate. Although ability grouping continues to predominate in middle level schools, a general decrease in the practice has occurred. In general, all grade 5–8 schools use less ability grouping than schools with 7–8–9 grade configurations. The practice of grouping by ability for the gifted remains common. On the whole, the survey results indicate that gifted programs have increased since the 1981 study.

Instructional Issues

During the last two decades, learning theorists have produced important research to help educators better understand the processes of learning. Other research indicates, however, that little has changed at the heart of middle level schools (Irvin, 1992). Questions on specific innovative classroom practices such as literature-based language arts programs, or cooperative learning, were beyond the scope of this survey, but organizational issues such as teacher-to-pupil ratio, grading practices, and length of the instructional period clearly frame the dynamics of the classroom. We address these organizational elements of instruction in this section.

❑ Teacher-to-Pupil Ratio

Eight alternatives were provided for principals to estimate classroom teacher-to-pupil ratio for the current school year. Table 3.18 shows that most middle level principals (42 percent) reported a ratio of one teacher for 21 to 25 students, followed by one teacher for 26 to 30 students (33 percent). All grade level organizations indicated these ratios, with the exception of schools containing grades 7–8–9. Most often, teacher-to-pupil ratio was one teacher for 26 to 30 students in those schools.

No significant differences in teacher-to-pupil ratio were found between the present study and 1981.

TABLE 3.18
Teacher/Pupil Ratio by Grade Level Organization

	Total	7–8–9	7–8	6–7–8	5–6–7–8	Other
10 or fewer	1	0	0	1	3	0
11–15	4	2	4	6	0	0
16–20	14	13	11	16	20	7
21–25	42	38	48	39	47	47
26–30	33	40	37	31	27	23
31–35	6	7	0	7	3	23

❏ Grade Reporting Procedures

Systems used by schools to report academic performance have been criticized for many years. The conventional report card with marks or grades falls short of being a developmentally appropriate procedure for reporting the academic performance or progress of middle grade students (Vars, 1992). Mac Iver (1990) stated that virtually all (99 percent) schools with grade 7 give students letter or number grades for each subject.

Many middle level educators are considering alternate formats that reflect an awareness of the unique characteristics of the young adolescent learner. Responsive reporting practices accommodate individual differences, contribute to positive student self-concept, facilitate student self-evaluation, and promote positive relationships among peers.

This study shows that the letter scale remains the most prevalent method of reporting. Table 3.19 summarizes grade reporting procedures by grade level. Principals cited *all* grade reporting procedures for the basic subjects of language arts, math, science, and social studies.

TABLE 3.19
Grade Reporting Procedures by Grade Level

	Grade				
	5	6	7	8	9
Letter scale	70	78	81	79	83
Word scale, e.g., excellent, good	13	16	14	14	15
Number scale	3	10	10	10	12
S/U, pass-fail	30	32	28	25	22
Informal written notes	30	36	31	30	24
Percentage marks	27	25	21	22	5
Progress in relation to potential	17	16	11	10	5
Other	7	7	7	7	2

Educational Programs

Satisfactory-unsatisfactory or pass-fail, informal written notes, and percentage marks were used to a significant degree at all grade levels. No important differences were found in grade reporting procedures between grade levels, but letter grades and number scales increased as students moved to higher grade levels, and progress reported in relationship to potential decreased.

Few schools reported progress in relation to student potential. These findings are similar to Mac Iver's 1990 study that found 19 percent of schools with seventh graders used progress grades (17 percent in this study). Approximately one-third of the principals reported that their schools used informal written notes with personal comments about student performance, effort, conduct, and so forth.

❏ The Instructional Period

Middle level schools employ various methods for academic scheduling (e.g., block, modular, flexible), but most schools utilize a specific number of daily periods. Principals were asked about the number of instructional periods and the length of the basic period.

Almost half the principals reported 7 instructional periods with 41 to 45 minutes per period (Tables 3.20 and 3.21). Only 1 percent of the schools surveyed used 5 periods; another 1 percent used a 56–60 minute period. A few schools had 9 or 10 periods per day.

TABLE 3.20

Number of Instructional Periods by Grade Level Organization

	Total	7–8–9	7–8	6–7–8	5–6–7–8	Other
5 periods	1	0	0	3	0	0
6 periods	21	34	28	14	13	31
7 periods	49	41	46	55	42	46
8 periods	24	23	22	23	32	23
Other	5	2	4	5	13	0

TABLE 3.21

Length of Instructional Period by Grade Level Organization

	Total	7–8–9	7–8	6–7–8	5–6–7–8	Other
40 minutes	9	3	13	9	13	8
41–45 min.	42	27	35	47	55	46
46–50 min.	25	32	22	25	13	15
51–55 min.	23	38	30	18	16	23
56–60 min.	1	0	0	1	3	8

Twenty-four percent of the schools employed eight-period days, with 5–6–7–8 schools most often implementing this practice. Epstein and Mac Iver (1990), in surveying future practices, predicted that in three years from their study, the number of middle level schools with an eight-period day would increase by 30 to 40 percent.

For the most part, few changes have occurred in teacher-pupil ratio and grade reporting procedures since the 1981 study. Teacher-to-pupil ratio has remained about one teacher for 21 to 25 students, and letter grades continue to predominate for reporting student progress. Almost half the schools have seven instructional periods daily, but many are implementing eight-period schedules.

Curriculum

Middle level scholars contend that curricular reforms have taken a back seat to organizational changes in school restructuring (Beane, 1990; Brazee, 1989; Toefper, 1992). This suggests that we have been more concerned with *how* we teach than with *what* we teach.

An Agenda for Excellence (NASSP, 1984) addressed content and organization of curriculum for young adolescents. The authors recommended a balance between skill development and content coverage that would allow students to connect materials and skills and transfer knowledge to other subject areas. *An Agenda for Excellence* strongly recommended content relevant to the immediate concerns of the young adolescent learner. *Turning Points* (Carnegie, 1989) asserted that "every middle grade school should offer a core academic program and should expect every student to complete that program successfully" (p. 42).

❑ Content Areas Required and Elective

As in the 1981 NASSP study, principals were given a listing of courses and asked to check those required in their schools and those available as electives. The 1992 survey results (Table 3.22) showed once again that English/language arts, mathematics, science, social studies, reading, and physical education are the most commonly offered content areas.

New content areas, listed for the first time on this study, included sex education, computer education, study skills, agriculture, journalism, and creative education. Principals also wrote in content areas offered as exploratory or elective, such as biracial communication, metal and woodworking, departmental guidance, cultural highlights, technology education, newspaper, and "problem solving." (The majority of principals, assistant principals, and members of leadership teams have rated required exploratory opportunities as "very important" to an instructionally effective middle level school. See Table 3.14.)

Table 3.23 shows the differences between the 1981 and 1992 studies for required course offerings by selected content areas. It is interesting to note the general decrease in percentages of schools requiring courses, especially for grades 5 and 6. However, a slight increase was evident for science and social studies in grades 7–8–9. Science is now required 10 percent more often in grade 9 than it was in 1981. Mathematics and physical education also are now required more often in grade 9.

TABLE 3.22

Content Areas "Required" and/or "Elective"

Subject	Grade 5 R	5 E	6 R	6 E	7 R	7 E	8 R	8 E	9 R	9 E
English/ Lang. Arts	85	18	95	9	97	3	95	4	96	7
Mathematics	85	21	96	8	97	2	96	3	93	2
Science	85	21	97	9	97	2	95	4	82	14
Social Science	85	21	97	9	97	2	96	3	86	9
Reading	82	21	86	9	65	18	57	23	16	39
Physical Education	85	18	96	10	94	4	88	12	77	18
Health Education	67	18	73	7	70	5	66	7	46	7
Sex Education	42	12	47	11	51	8	49	11	36	7
Spelling	76	15	72	6	53	6	53	6	27	7
Typing/Keyboarding	33	9	37	17	24	27	14	38	7	59
Computer Education	46	21	42	17	38	27	29	43	9	59
Art	76	12	62	27	47	43	32	57	2	86
Crafts	3	6	5	11	4	22	3	24	2	46
Foreign Language	3	9	15	13	14	34	10	52	9	77
Family Living Home Econ.	12	9	27	11	30	27	19	46	0	73
Industrial Education	21	12	31	17	40	34	26	54	0	91
Vocal Music	24	21	23	34	14	53	10	57	0	84
Chorus	6	30	7	51	3	64	3	69	0	75
Instrumental Music	12	55	6	74	3	86	3	85	0	93
Orchestra	3	15	3	37	1	45	1	44	0	55
General Music	42	12	39	23	26	27	15	22	0	21
Speech	3	0	3	7	3	14	3	18	2	39
Drama	0	6	4	18	2	27	2	35	0	48
Career Education	9	3	8	7	9	10	11	12	7	27
Study Skills	15	0	25	10	23	13	18	13	0	25
Agriculture	6	3	1	4	1	5	0	7	0	25
Journalism	0	0	1	4	0	11	0	25	0	57
Creative Education	0	0	0	2	0	4	0	5	0	5
Photography	0	0	1	5	8	9	1	11	0	25
Other	3	3	1	2	2	2	1	3	0	5

TABLE 3.23

Comparison of Required Content Areas—1992 and 1981 NASSP Studies

	Grade 5		Grade 6		Grade 7		Grade 8		Grade 9	
	'92	'81	'92	'81	'92	'81	'92	'81	'92	'81
English/Lang. Arts	85	100	95	100	97	99	95	98	96	96
Mathematics	85	100	96	100	97	99	96	98	93	92
Science	85	100	97	99	97	93	95	93	82	72
Social Studies	85	93	97	97	97	96	96	93	86	80
Reading	82	98	86	95	65	72	57	60	16	26
Physical Educ.	85	95	96	99	94	96	88	91	77	33

Reading remains an important content area, but like most other subjects, it is required somewhat less of the time. Becker (1990) found that 85 percent of middle grade schools provide a course in reading separate from language arts. Reading as a required subject decreases as students move through the grades.

Of the schools that used interdisciplinary team organization to deliver instruction, 51 percent had reading as a teamed subject. Teams that include reading may emphasize the integration of learning and study skills strategies with the teaching of content. However, systematic reading instruction in middle level schools is often reserved for remedial students or offered only among the exploratory courses (Irvin and Connors, 1989b).

Instrumental music was the most popular elective for all grade levels in the 1981 study and in the current study, with indications of a slight increase in popularity.

❏ Organizational Formats for Subjects

Many middle level education experts hold that traditional organizational formats such as self-contained classroom and period-by-period/departmentalized instruction do not offer young adolescents flexible enough learning environments. Principals were asked to identify the organizational format (self-contained classroom, interdisciplinary teaming, period-by-period/departmentalized instruction, or disciplinary teaming) used to teach the majority of students at each grade level for five primary subject areas. Results (Table 3.24) indicated no significant differences in the organizational formats of English/language arts, mathematics, science, social science, and reading.

Interdisciplinary teaming was slightly more common than self-contained classrooms as the primary instructional format for the fifth grade in all subject areas. Interdisciplinary teaming was the primary format for instruction for all subjects in the sixth grade, followed by period-by-period/departmentalized instruction. Almost half of all sixth grades used interdisciplinary teaming for all subject areas. Grades seven, eight, and nine generally used period-by-period/ departmentalized organization for instruction, followed by teaming. The frequency of interdisciplinary team organization decreases (and departmentalization increases) as students move through the grades.

Educational Programs

TABLE 3.24

Organizational Format for Subject Areas by Grade Level Organization

	English/ Lang. Arts					Mathematics					Science					Social Sci.					Reading				
Grade	5	6	7	8	9	5	6	7	8	9	5	6	7	8	9	5	6	7	8	9	5	6	7	8	9
Not Taught	0	0	<1	<1	0	0	0	<1	<1	0	0	0	<1	<1	0	0	<1	<1	<1	0	2	2	9	12	22
Self Contained Class	36	17	6	5	5	33	13	5	5	8	33	13	5	5	8	33	16	6	5	6	37	18	7	5	6
Interdisciplinary Teaming	37	46	35	30	8	27	45	32	26	11	35	46	32	28	6	37	47	35	30	7	33	44	28	25	6
Period–by–Period Departmentalized	22	31	55	61	82	26	35	59	64	85	27	36	59	69	85	25	32	55	61	83	22	30	53	56	66
Disciplinary Teaming	5	6	3	4	4	6	6	3	3	1	5	5	3	3	1	5	5	3	3	4	6	6	3	2	0

Although there has been a slight decrease in schools requiring some content areas, the variety of courses and electives still offered suggests a broad-based curriculum. The increase in interdisciplinary teaming implies that curricular integration is increasingly a higher priority for middle level educators.

Cocurricular Activities

Structured student activities outside the formal realm of curriculum and instruction give students additional opportunities for peer and adult interaction, exploration of interests, appropriate use of leisure time, and scope beyond basic curriculum offerings. These activities are often scheduled during the regular school day, but may take place after school, in the evenings, or on weekends.

Principals, assistant principals, and members of leadership teams were asked how important the cocurricular program was to an instructionally effective middle level school (see Table 3.15). Forty-six percent of principals, 40 percent of assistant principals, and 42 percent of the leadership team members rated cocurricular activities as "very important." At the other extreme, many principals (37 percent) reported no cocurricular programs in their schools and no plans to implement them.

Principals were asked about the grade levels at which students were permitted to participate in various cocurricular activities. Table 3.25 presents 10 activities and the respective percentages for participation at each grade level. Students are allowed more participation in every cocurricular activity as they progress through the grade levels. Principals also said their schools offered intramurals and interscholastic sports as cocurricular activities.

TABLE 3.25

Cocurricular Activities by Grade Levels

Activity	5	6	7	8	9
Career Days	15	35	38	57	57
Debate	6	9	11	16	27
Drama	15	35	46	53	59
Honor Societies	3	20	41	48	68
Intramural Sports	61	74	73	70	68
Mini-courses	15	25	27	25	7
Musical Groups	58	78	85	86	91
Publications	36	41	56	75	84
Student Clubs	49	74	82	82	84
Student Government	67	83	91	92	100
Other	0	4	5	7	9

Interscholastic Sports

Proponents of appropriate physical education for middle level students contend that interscholastic sports can result in physical as well as emotional injury to young adolescents. Of primary concern are the risks of permanent bone and joint damage in certain sports. Interscholastic programs generally prevail in middle level schools because parents and communities, more than educational leaders, support them. In the current survey, 43 percent of principals, 42 percent of assistant principals, and 37 percent of leadership team members said that intramural rather than interscholastic activities should be emphasized in all middle grades (see Table 3.21).

Some educators believe that well-designed intramural programs provide adequately for *all* students, not just the athletically talented. Intramural programs emphasize exercise, enjoyment, and social skills over competitiveness. More than half the principals (58 percent) said that intramural activities for all students were "very important."

Seventy-two percent said they were planning or considering implementation of intramurals in the next two years (see Table 3.15).

Principals were asked about the grade levels at which boys and girls in their schools were permitted to participate in various interscholastic sports. The data in Tables 3.26 and 3.27 indicate that interscholastic sports are strong in middle level schools despite opposition by many middle level educators. In comparing their 1968 and 1988 surveys, Alexander and McEwin (1989) found that girls' interscholastic sports had increased a minimum of 27 percent to a maximum of 55 percent in grades 6, 7, and 8. The respective increases for boys ranged from 25 to 27 percent. The present study corroborated these increases.

Educational Programs

TABLE 3.26

Boys' Interscholastic Sports by Grade Level

	Grade				
	5	6	7	8	9
No Inter. Sport	62	39	9	7	0
Have. Inter. Sport	38	61	91	93	100
Baseball	0	8	21	22	58
Basketball	5	23	79	85	95
Football	3	5	49	57	86
Gymnastics	0	< 1	2	2	7
Ice Hockey	0	0	1	1	14
Soccer	5	10	23	24	51
Softball	0	5	5	6	12
Swimming	5	5	9	11	33
Tennis	3	4	15	16	58
Track	5	17	63	67	86
Volleyball	3	5	8	10	19
Wrestling	5	11	38	40	67
Other	0	5	12	12	14

TABLE 3.27

Girls' Interscholastic Sports by Grade Level

	Grade				
	5	6	7	8	9
No Inter. Sport	62	39	9	6	0
Have. Inter. Sport	38	61	91	94	100
Baseball	0	3	5	5	7
Basketball	5	22	77	82	91
Football	0	< 1	7	10	16
Gymnastics	0	2	7	7	21
Ice Hockey	0	0	0	0	2
Soccer	5	9	22	23	51
Softball	3	12	26	27	56
Swimming	5	5	10	11	30
Tennis	3	4	15	16	58
Track	5	17	62	66	84
Volleyball	3	14	51	57	74
Wrestling	3	1	4	4	7
Other	0	4	13	14	19

As students progress to the higher grades, they are allowed more participation in interscholastic sports. Increasing participation from one grade to the next is generally similar for boys and girls.

Consistent with the results of the 1981 survey, this study showed that basketball and track were the most popular sports at all grade levels for both boys and girls. (Boys' track tied with football in grade 9.) Generally, football was next for boys and volleyball for girls. Wrestling, baseball, and soccer for boys, and softball, soccer, and tennis for girls were also popular activities.

Traditionally, middle level schools have provided between-school competition for boys. Table 3.28 compares interscholastic sports for boys in grades 7 and 8 by school grade level configurations. The results show that 6–7–8 and 5–6–7–8 schools implemented somewhat fewer interscholastic sports programs than 7–8–9 and 7–8 schools. The differences are not large, but the trend is clear. Schools clearly configured for the middle supported fewer interscholastic sports activities.

TABLE 3.28
Boys' Interscholastic Sports by Grade Pattern (Seventh and Eighth Grade)

	7–8–9	6–7–8	5–6–7–8	7–8
Grade 7				
Interscholastic Sports	95	89	91	94
No Interscholastic Sports	5	11	9	6
Grade 8				
Interscholastic Sports	97	92	94	100
No Interscholastic Sports	3	8	6	0

It also would appear that middle level schools are increasing the variety of interscholastic sports programs. Principals indicated that cross country, field hockey, golf, bowling, cheerleading, flag football, lacrosse, and even fencing are available to students.

Summary

The results of this study, as well as the findings of other contemporary national studies, provide evidence of the increase in programs and practices responsive to the nature and needs of early adolescents.

During the last decade, schools have increased the use of interdisciplinary team organization. Fifty-seven percent of the principals surveyed indicated that their schools employed teams of teachers and students. Teaming was most often used in the lower grades and by schools with a 6–7–8 grade configuration. Teaming schools reported that 76 to 100 percent of their students received instruction from interdisciplinary teams.

Principals reported that 37 percent of team leaders were appointed by the administration; 40 percent were selected by the team membership; and 32 percent rotated the leader responsibility. Ten percent of team leaders were given released time and 27 percent were compensated for leader responsibilities. Thirty-five percent of the principals whose schools had teaming reported that one planning period was provided at the same time, for all members of a team. Fifty-four percent reported one common planning period for all team members plus an individual planning period.

Middle level schools continue to examine their procedures for grouping students. Eighty-two percent of the schools said they used some form of ability grouping. Almost 70 percent grouped students into specific classes by ability, and 13 percent said that teachers grouped students within classes.

Indications by principals suggested some decrease in ability grouping. Thirty-six percent of those currently grouping students by academic ability were considering eliminating the practice. On the other hand, since 1981, 15 percent more middle level schools offer programs for gifted or talented students.

The letter scale is overwhelmingly the predominant method for reporting pupil progress. Little difference was found in grade reporting procedures between grade levels, except that informal written notes and progress reported in relation to potential were employed slightly more often in the lower grades.

Almost half the principals reported seven periods per day in their schools. Forty-one to 45-minute periods were most common. Twenty-four percent had an eight-period day.

During the last decade, schools have increased the use of interdisciplinary team organization. Fifty-seven percent of the principals surveyed indicated that their schools employed teams of teachers and students.

English/language arts, mathematics, science, social studies, reading, and physical education remained important content areas for the middle grades. There has been a general decrease in percentages of schools requiring content areas, especially in the lower grades. Instrumental music has persisted as the most popular elective.

No significant differences in organizational format for teaching were found among the subjects of English/language arts, mathematics, science, social science, and reading. The fifth grade used the self-contained classroom more often; interdisciplinary teaming was the primary format in the sixth grade. Grades 7, 8, and 9 used period-by-period/departmentalized organization.

Principals reported that their schools offered more participation in cocurricular activities as students progressed through the grade levels. Interscholastic sports continued as a primary activity in middle level schools. Participation was highest in the upper middle level grades. Principals said that basketball and track were the most popular sports for boys and girls at all grade levels.

Issues and Trends

T he perceptions and opinions of principals, assistant principals, and leadership team members on important issues and trends in middle level education are reported in this chapter. Data are organized under the following topics: tasks of American schools, school organization, leadership and management, school program, personnel, and outreach.

Tasks of American Schools

Principals, assistant principals, and leadership team members, when asked to rank what they believed to be the important tasks of American schools, showed strong agreement in ranking "acquisition of basic skills," "development of positive self-concept and human relations skills," "development of skills in critical inquiry and problem solving," and "preparation for a changing world" as first through fourth, respectively (Table 4.1).

Differences were evident in the perceptions of the three groups about the ranking of "development of skills for a technological society," "knowledge about skills in preparation for family life," and "development of moral and spiritual values," but these differences were minor. All three groups ranked these tasks within the five to seven range.

"Understanding of the American value system," "career planning and training in beginning occupational skills," "physical fitness," and "appreciation for and experience with the arts" were ranked 8 through 11 by all three groups.

Comparisons of rankings of these same 11 tasks by middle level and high school principals in all NASSP studies (NASSP Middle Level Studies 1992, 1981, and 1966, and NASSP High School Studies 1988, 1978, and 1965) yielded some interesting findings (Table 4.2). Principals in all six studies ranked acquisition of basic skills first. Development of positive self-concept and human relations skills was ranked second in the 1992 and 1981 middle level studies, and in the 1988 and 1978 high school studies, moving up from a ranking of sixth in the 1966 middle level study and

TABLE 4.1

Tasks of American Schools—Rankings by Middle Level Principals, Assistant Principals, and Leadership Team Members

Tasks	Principals	Assistant Principals	Leadership Team Members
Acquisition of basic skills (reading, writing, speaking, computing, etc.)	1	1	1
Development of positive self-concept and good human relations	2	2	2
Development of skills and practice in critical intellectual inquiry and problem solving	3	3	3
Preparation for a changing world	4	4	4
Development of skills to function in a technological society (engineering, scientific, etc.)	5	5	6
Knowledge about and skills in preparation for family life (sex education, home management, problems of aging, etc.)	6	7	5
Development of moral and spiritual values	7	6	7
Understanding of the American value system (its political, economic, social values, etc.)	8	8	8
Career planning and training in beginning occupational skills	9	9	9
Physical fitness and useful leisure time sports	10	10	10
Appreciation for and experience with the fine arts	11	11	11

seventh in the 1965 high school study. In addition, preparation for a changing world shifted upward to fourth in the rankings from seventh (middle level) and eighth (high school).

Middle level principals in this study ranked the development of skills to function in a technological society much higher than in 1981, and higher than high school principals in 1988. It is also interesting to note the drop in the ranking of the development of moral and spiritual values, from second in 1965/66 to seventh (middle level) and fifth (high school) in the current study.

School Organizational Issues

❑ Ideal Grade Level Organization

For more than 30 years, middle level educators have been debating the "ideal" grade level pattern for developmentally appropriate middle level schools. Findings from the 1981 NASSP study showed that more than half the principals favored a 6–7–8 grade level configuration. This trend

TABLE 4.2

Tasks of American Schools—Comparisons with Previous NASSP Middle Level and High School Studies

Tasks	ML Principals			HS Principals		
	1992	1981	1966	1987	1977	1965
Acquisition of basic skills (reading, writing, speaking, computing, etc).	1	1	1	1	1	1
Development of positive self-concept and good human relations	2	2	6	2	2	7
Development of skills and practice in critical intellectual inquiry and problem solving	3	3	4.5	3	3	4
Preparation for a changing world	4	7	–	3	3	4
Development of skills to function in a techno-logical society (engineering, scientific, etc.)	5	10	9	8	10	8
Knowledge about and skills in preparation for family life (sex education, home management, problems of aging, etc.)	6	8	–	9	6	–
Development of moral and spiritual values	7	4	2	–	–	–
Understanding of the American value system (its political, economic, social values, etc.)	8	5	4.5	7	7	3
Career planning and training in beginning occupational skills	9	6	–	6	5	–
Physical fitness and useful leisure time sports	10	9	8	10	9	6
Appreciation for and experience with the fine arts	11	11	–	11	11	–

has continued with principals, assistant principals, and leadership team members all showing strong preference for this grade level organization (Table 4.3). In fact, a much higher percentage of the 1992 principals (72 percent) indicated preference for this structure than did those in the 1981 study (54 percent).

TABLE 4.3

Opinions About Ideal Grade Level Organization—Principals, Assistant Principals, and Leadership Team Members

	1992			1981
	Principals	Assistant Principals	Leadership Team Members	Principals
7–8–9	6	8	9	17
7–8	12	20	17	18
6–7–8	72	59	65	54
5–6–7–8	7	5	5	6
Other	3	8	4	5

The preference for grade 6–7–8 middle level schools is the choice of a majority of middle level principals regardless of the grade level configurations of their present schools (Table 4.4). As might be expected, the highest percentage of principals favoring the 6–7–8 structure were those assigned to 6–7–8 schools. Although a majority of principals in 5–6–7–8 schools showed support for the 6–7–8 structure, they also strongly favored (44 percent) their current grade level structures.

TABLE 4.4

Principal Opinions About Ideal Grade Level Organization—Comparison by Grade Level Organization of Principals' Current School

		Current School Organization				
	Total	7–8–9	7–8	6–7–8	5–6–7–8	Other
7–8–9	6	15	9	3	0	0
7–8	12	18	24	10	3	0
6–7–8	72	62	65	80	53	100
5–6–7–8	7	5	0	3	44	0
Other	3	0	2	4	0	0

❏ Changing Grade Level Structures

Sixty-five percent of the respondents in this study reported that their schools had moved to a 5–6–7–8 or 6–7–8 grade level configuration, a much higher figure than the 25 percent that reported the change in 1981 (table 4.5). This trend is representative of the nationwide tendency to add the sixth grade and, less frequently, the fifth grade to the middle school. As a result, the 6–7–8 grade pattern has emerged as the most common configuration in American middle level education (Alexander and McEwin, 1989).

TABLE 4.5

Principals Report on Changing Grade Level Structures

Schools that changed to a 5–6–7–8 or 6–7–8 grade configuration	1992	1981
Yes	65	25
No	35	75

Middle level principals whose schools have changed to a 5–6–7–8 or 6–7–8 pattern reported that the primary reason for the change was to "provide a program best suited to meet the needs of the middle level age student" (Table 4.6). The number of principals giving this reason is up 25 percentage points from the 1981 study. Only one-third of the principals in this study reported that the grade levels of their schools were changed to adjust for enrollment trends, so it appears that middle schools are being modified to solve enrollment problems less frequently.

FIGURE 4.3

Opinions About Ideal Grade Level Organization—Principals, Assistant Principals, and Leadership Team Members

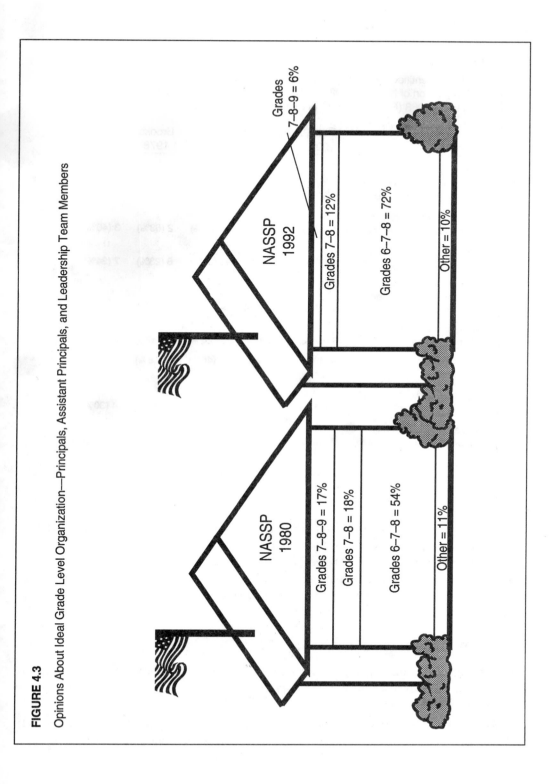

TABLE 4.6

Reasons Identified by Principals for Changing to 5–6–7–8 or 6–7–8 Configuration: A Comparison of NASSP 1992, Alexander 1989, NASSP 1981, Brooks 1978, and Alexander 1968 (Rankings and Percentages of Response)

Reasons for Change	NASSP 1992	Alexander 1989	NASSP 1981	Brooks 1978	Alexander 1968
Provide a program best suited to the needs of the middle level age student	1 (86%)	1 (65%)	1 (61%)	1 (68%)	2 (45%)
Provide a better transition from elem. to high school	2 (82%)	2 (51%)	2 (57%)	2 (63%)	3 (40%)
Employ new curriculum or instructional innovations	3 (60%)	6 (21%)	4 (31%)	6 (23%)	7 (24%)
Employ ideas or programs successfully implemented in other schools	4 (48%)	9 (14%)	9 (17%)	9 (13%)	9 (13%)
Solve concerns about a junior high program	5 (47%)	4 (29%)	7 (24%)	4 (26%)	5 (25%)
Adjust to enrollment needs	6 (33%)	3 (50%)	3 (46%)	3 (48%)	1 (58%)
Provide fifth and/or sixth graders with more curricular specialization	7 (31%)	8 (16%)	6 (26%)	7 (20%)	4 (30%)
Move ninth graders into the high school program	8 (29%)	5 (39%)	8 (19%)	5 (29%)	5 (25%)
Utilize a new school facility or building	9 (20%)	7 (18%)	5 (28%)	8 (18%)	8 (20%)

Also of consequence is the greater percentage of schools that changed grade pattern to "employ ideas or programs successfully implemented in other middle level schools." This motive, which was identified by 48 percent of the principals, moved from ninth in previous studies to fourth in this study. Finally and significantly, "employing new curriculum or instructional innovations" received a higher ranking in each successive middle level study, moving from seventh in Alexander's 1968 study to third in this study.

❑ Optimum School Size

Sixty-eight percent of the middle level administrators in this study indicated that optimal enrollment for a middle level school was in the range of 400–799 students (combined categories 400–599 and 600–799) (See Table 4.7).

This range of enrollment was supported by a majority of all principals, regardless of the grade level structures of their school. The largest number of respondents supported the 400–599 category.

TABLE 4.7

Principal Opinions About Ideal Enrollment—Comparison by Grade Level
Organization of Principals' Current School

Enrollment	Total	Current School Organization				
		7–8–9	7–8	6–7–8	5–6–7–8	Other
Fewer than 200	2	0	0	3	3	0
200–399	16	8	15	16	24	23
400–599	41	38	44	39	59	67
600–799	27	38	28	26	7	0
800–999	9	16	13	9	0	0
1,000–1,399	5	0	0	7	7	0
More than 1,400	0	0	0	0	0	0

Principals and assistant principals in this study showed strong agreement about ideal enrollment, both supporting the 400–799 range (Table 4.8). The 1981 study also endorsed this enrollment range, but principal level of support was a bit lower at 63 percent, compared to 68 percent for 1992.

TABLE 4.8

Principal Opinions About Ideal Enrollment—Comparison of 1992 Principals and
Assistant Principals and 1981 Principals

Enrollment	1992		1981
	Principals	Assistant Principals	Principals
200	2	0	—
200–399	16	12	12
400–599	41	45	27
600–799	27	28	36
800–999	9	5	17
1,000–1,399	5	4	8
1,400	0	0	0

❏ Administrative Use of Technology

Dramatic increases have occurred in the administrative use of technology since the 1981 middle level study. In that earlier study, 42 percent of the principals said they did not have access to information processing equipment. Those with access used it for scheduling (50 percent), grade reporting (46 percent), and record keeping (36 percent).

In 1992, 88 percent of the principals reported they used some form of technology for administrative purposes (Table 4.9). Most frequently mentioned uses were maintaining student records on attendance (88 percent), preparing grade reports (87 percent), preparing written communications such as brochures and newsletters (85 percent), and scheduling classes (83 percent).

TABLE 4.9

Administrative Use of Technology

Uses	Total
Maintaining student records on attendance	88
Preparing grade reports	87
Preparing written communication such as brochures and newsletters	85
Scheduling classes	83
Processing correspondence and meeting other basic office operational needs	71
Facilitating operations in the library/media center	66
Maintaining fiscal records	58
Assisting teachers in the preparation and development of tests and teaching materials	54
Maintaining student records on disciplinary behaviors	52
Scoring teacher-made tests	49
Maintaining personnel records	41
Interactive communication device with other professionals	32
Selecting samples for student or parent surveys	22
Interactive communication device to identify and retrieve instructional materials	20
Providing a hot-line information service to persons who call the school	15
Providing computer-base telephone messages to the home (e.g., to notify parents of student absences)	13
Other	2

Leadership and Management Issues

❏ Leadership Style

The current literature on administrative functions makes a clear distinction between leadership and management. Leaders are expected to be visionary, with the capacity to inspire, to create positive working environments, and to enable employees to reach full potential as productive members of the organization. On the other hand, managers are understood to direct day-to-day operations, overseeing all the details needed to ensure a smooth running, functioning workplace. Educational administrators, like many administrators in the private sector, are constantly faced with the conflicting demands of leadership and management, and must function in the dual roles of visionary and organizer.

When presented with the choice of effectively and efficiently managing the day-to-day operation of the school or providing leadership for the school based upon his or her best professional judgment, middle level principals indicated a strong preference for the leadership role (Table 4.10). Female principals showed the stronger preference for the leadership option at 90 percent, compared to 81 percent of the male respondents.

TABLE 4.10

Principal Opinions About Management/Leadership

	Total	Male	Female
Principal should effectively and efficiently manage the day-by-day operation of the school	18	19	10
Principal should provide leadership for the school based upon his/her best professional judgment	82	81	90

❑ Shared Decision Making

There was almost unanimous agreement that principals should share the decision-making process with the faculty on important school issues (Table 4.11). Ninety-eight percent of both male and female principals indicated a strong commitment to shared decision making.

TABLE 4.11

Principal Opinions About Shared Decision Making

	Total	Male	Female
Principal should establish agenda and decide the important issues in the school	2	2	2
Principal should share the decision making with the faculty on important school issues	98	98	98

❑ Representation and School Policy

Whose interests should the principal represent? What initiative should he or she take in developing and implementing policy? Thirty-eight percent of the respondents indicated that principals should primarily represent the interest of parents, leaders, and patrons of the schools (Table 4.12).

Sixty-two percent, however, believed that principals should take the initiative in developing and implementing school policy according to his or her best professional judgment. A greater number of male administrators (62 to 55 percent) appeared to favor taking the initiative; a higher percentage of female principals (45 to 37 percent) favored representing the interests of parents, leaders, and patrons of the school.

TABLE 4.12

Principal Opinions About School Policy

	Total	Male	Female
Principal primarily should represent the interest of parents, leaders, and patrons of the school	38	37	45
Principal should take the initiative in developing and implementing school policy according to his/her best professional judgment	62	63	55

❑ Perceived Roadblocks

Principals, assistant principals, and leadership team members were given a list of 26 factors that could be considered "roadblocks" preventing principals from doing the job they wished to do. Respondents were asked to indicate the degree to which each factor has or has not been a roadblock during the past two years. Analysis of the data showed that two-thirds of the principals identified 10 factors as either "moderate" or "extreme" roadblocks. Eight factors were identified by two-thirds of the assistant principals, and 7 by two-thirds of the leadership team members.

The following factors were cited by two-thirds of the principals as either moderate or extreme roadblocks.

- Inability to obtain funding (86 percent)
- Time taken by administrative detail at the expense of more important matters (85 percent)
- Lack of time for myself (80 percent)
- Regulations/mandates from state/district governing boards (79 percent)
- Inability to provide teacher time for planning or professional development (74 percent)
- Resistance to change (73 percent)
- Variations in the ability and dedication of staff (71 percent)
- Parents apathetic or irresponsible about their children (71 percent)
- Lack of knowledge among staff regarding program for middle level students (68 percent)
- Insufficient space and physical facilities (66 percent).

Factors identified by two-thirds of the assistant principals as either moderate or extreme roadblocks for principals included the following.

- Problem students (79 percent)
- Resistance to change (78 percent)
- Parents apathetic or irresponsible about their children (77 percent)

- Variations in the ability and dedication of staff (76 percent)
- Time taken by administrative detail at expense of more important matters (75 percent)
- Lack of time for self (74 percent)
- Inability to obtain funding (67 percent)
- Regulations/mandates from state/district governing boards (66 percent).

Two-thirds of the leadership team members reported the following moderate or extreme road-blocks to effective principal leadership:

- Inability to obtain funding (82 percent)
- Parents apathetic or irresponsible about their children (80 percent)
- Problem students (77 percent)
- Resistance to change (75 percent)
- Lack of time for self (74 percent)
- Variations in the ability and dedication of staff (72 percent)
- Inability to provide teacher time for planning or professional development (68 percent).

Five of these roadblocks were identified as moderate or extreme by two-thirds of the principals, assistant principals, and leadership team members. These included: inability to obtain funding, lack of time for myself, resistance to change, variations in the ability and dedication of staff, and parents apathetic or irresponsible about their children. Inability to obtain funding was clearly the consensus roadblock here, but assistant principals and leadership team members ranked apathetic parents almost as high. Principals apparently have had better experiences with parents, or have had to deal less often with the more irresponsible among them. Principals lack of time for self was the consensus second choice among the top five, suggesting that the busy nature of the job is evident to all.

In the 1981 study, two-thirds of the principals identified the following factors as roadblocks: time taken by administrative detail (86 percent), apathetic or irresponsible parents (78 percent), problem students (77 percent), inability to obtain funding (75 percent), lack of time for myself (75 percent), variations in the ability and dedication of staff (74 percent), and resistance to change by staff (69 percent). The differences between the perceived roadblocks of 1981 principals and 1992 principals are minor. "Problem students," which received the second highest percentage (77 percent) in 1981, was 64 percent in the 1992 study and did not record the two-thirds needed to be identified as a major roadblock. "Apathetic parents" at the top in the 1981 listing of factors was replaced by "inability to obtain funding" in the 1992 study.

School Program Issues

❑ Instructionally Effective Middle Level Schools

Principals, assistant principals, and leadership team members were asked to assess the importance of five programs considered by middle level experts to be of benefit to early adolescents (Table 4.14): interdisciplinary teams, exploratory courses, adviser/advisee programs, cocurricular programs, and intramural activities.

TABLE 4.13

Perceptions of Principals, Assistant Principals, and Leadership Team Members About Roadblocks That Prevent Principals from Doing the Kind of Job They Would Like To Do

Roadblocks	Principals			Assistant Principals			Leadership Team Members		
	Not a Factor	Moderate Factor	Extreme Factor	Not a Factor	Moderate Factor	Extreme Facto	Not a Factor	Moderate Factor	Extreme Factor
Collective Bargaining	41	40	19	69	22	9	67	27	6
Deficient communication among administrative levels	41	51	8	52	38	10	40	42	18
Inability to obtain funding	13	42	45	33	39	28	18	45	37
Inability to provide teacher time for planning or professional development	26	42	32	36	46	18	33	38	29
Insufficient space and physical facilities	34	39	27	37	39	24	40	36	24
Lack of competent administrative assistance	73	21	6	78	16	6	74	20	6
Lack of competent office help	81	15	4	73	21	6	85	12	3
Lack of data about student skills and styles	69	28	3	67	28	5	73	24	3
Lack of data on program successes/failures	64	34	2	60	33	7	62	34	4
Lack of districtwide flexibility (all schools conform to the same policy)	48	41	11	55	35	10	52	32	14
Lack of knowledge among staff regarding program for middle level students	34	52	14	41	44	15	42	45	13
Lack of time for myself	20	53	27	26	45	29	26	48	26
Long-standing tradition in the school/district	35	48	17	44	42	14	44	41	14

(continued)

TABLE 4.13 (CONTINUED)

Perceptions of Principals, Assistant Principals, and Leadership Team Members About Road-blocks That Prevent Principals from Doing the Kind of Job They Would Like To Do

Roadblocks	Principals			Assistant Principals			Leadership Team Members		
	Not a Factor	Moderate Factor	Extreme Factor	Not a Factor	Moderate Factor	Extreme Facto	Not a Factor	Moderate Factor	Extreme Factor
Parents apathetic or irresponsible about their children	29	46	25	23	41	36	20	44	36
Pressure from community	59	35	6	50	42	8	49	43	8
Problem students (apathetic, hostile, etc.)	31	42	22	21	49	30	23	55	22
Regulations/mandates from state/district governing boards	21	47	32	25	54	11	27	51	22
Resistance to change	27	52	21	22	54	24	25	55	20
Superintendent or central office staff	62	32	6	59	32	9	52	36	12
Teacher tenure	48	37	15	53	35	12	73	23	4
Teacher turnover	79	16	3	73	21	6	77	20	3
Time required to administer/ supervise cocurricular activities	37	51	12	47	42	11	58	34	8
Time taken by administrative detail at expense of more important matters	15	50	35	25	52	23	46	43	11
Too large a student body	69	22	9	54	28	18	67	21	12
Too small a student body	87	12	1	92	7	1	93	6	1
Variations in the ability and dedication of staff	29	58	13	24	53	23	28	58	14

Three-fourths of the principals, assistant principals, and leadership team members indicated that interdisciplinary teaming was "very important." Exploratory programs were also identified as very important by 77 percent of the principals, 68 percent of the assistant principals, and 70 percent of the leadership team members.

TABLE 4.14

Opinions About Characteristics Important to an Instructionally Effective Middle Level School by Principals, Assistant Principals, and Leadership Team Members

	Principals			Assistant Principals			Leadership Team Members		
	Importance								
Characteristic	1	2	3	1	2	3	1	2	3
Interdisciplinary teams of 2–5 teachers sharing common students, planning time, housed in close proximity	10	16	74	5	20	75	5	20	75
Exploratory course offerings that provide *required* (not elective) curricular opportunities for all students	4	19	77	4	28	68	3	27	70
Adviser-advisee program regularly scheduled for at least 15 minutes or more during each classroom day	17	28	55	13	45	42	17	46	37
Cocurricular program separate from regularly graded courses, but occurring during the school day, designed to provide students with the opportunity to pursue leadership roles, special interests, and socialization	16	38	46	7	53	40	8	50	42
Intramural activities offered for all students during or immediately after the regular classroom day	10	32	58	10	46	44	9	50	41

Importance of Characteristic:
1 - Little or no importance
2 - Somewhat important
3 - Very important

Although a majority of principals ranked adviser/advisee programs as very important, fewer than half the assistant principals (42 percent) and leadership team members (37 percent) rated them in the very important category. Adviser/advisee programs also received the highest number of "little or no importance" ratings from principals (16 percent), assistant principals (13 percent), and leadership team members (17 percent). These findings are indicative of the difficulty that some schools have had with the implementation and/or maintenance of adviser/advisee programs. It should be noted, however, that more than 80 percent of all the respondents did rank adviser/advisee programs as either "somewhat important" or "very important." Advisement is one of the most enduring program innovations of this century, as new research and best practice continues to establish (Jenkins, 1992).

Cocurricular programs occurring during the regular day and intramural activities offered during or immediately after the day received strong support from all three groups. Eighty-four percent of the principals, 93 percent of the assistant principals, and 92 percent of the leadership team members said that cocurricular activities were either somewhat important or very important. Similar levels of support were found for intramural activities, with more than 90 percent of principals, assistant principals, and leadership team members rating them somewhat or very important.

Principals were also asked to assess the level of current implementation of these five characteristics, and future plans for implementation at their school (Table 4.15). The exploratory program had the highest level of implementation (55 percent). This was followed by interdisciplinary teaming and intramural activities that were fully implemented in 36 percent of the schools. Fifty-one percent of the principals reported no implementation of adviser/advisee programs; 40 percent, no cocurricular programs; and a little more than a third, no interdisciplinary teaming.

Plans to fully implement exploratory programs were reported by 55 percent of the principals, followed by intramural programs at 40 percent of the respondents, and interdisciplinary teaming at 36 percent.

Thirty-seven percent of the principals said they intended to continue the same level of cocurricular activities for the next two years, and 30 percent said they would maintain the current level of adviser/advisee programs.

Although a high degree of support is clearly evident for these five characteristics/programs of instructionally effective middle level schools, it is also equally evident that, with the exception of exploratory courses, they have been fully implemented in less than 40 percent of middle level schools. Even more disheartening is the lack of implementation of interdisciplinary teaming in 36 percent of the schools and adviser/advisee programs in 51 percent. Indeed, too many schools have failed at implementation of advisement because of lack of administrative support, too short a timeline, too much group guidance, or teacher opposition. The time is ripe for a new look at this important practice in the clear light of current successes in the state of Florida and elsewhere.

❏ Ability Grouping

Grouping by ability, in spite of the research that shows its deleterious effect on early adolescents (Braddock, 1990; Oakes, 1985) still remains firmly entrenched in middle level schools (Braddock, 1990; Lounsbury and Clark, 1990). As reported earlier, ability grouping was found in 82 percent of the schools in this study (Chapter 3). It is no surprise, therefore, that ability grouping of students into certain classes is favored by a majority of principals, assistant principals, and leadership team members (Table 4.16). This type of grouping is different from the "tracking" of students for the entire day, but it is still inappropriate for most early adolescent learners (Braddock 1990; Oakes, 1985). Grouping students for instruction within a class, the most appropriate and defensible of the traditional grouping practices in middle level schools, was favored by fewer than one quarter of the principals (23 percent).

TABLE 4.15

Principal Opinions About the Characteristics of an Instructionally Effective Middle Level School—Importance, Current Implementation, Plans for Future Implementation

Characteristic	Importance of Characteristic			Current Implementation			Plans for Implementation				
	1	2	3	1	2	3	1	2	3	4	5
Interdisciplinary teams of 2–5 teachers sharing common students, planning time, housed in close proximity	10	16	74	36	27	36	36	2	16	22	24
Exploratory course offerings that provide *required* (not elective) curricular opportunities for all students	4	19	77	12	33	55	55	3	13	13	16
Adviser-advisee program regularly scheduled for at least 15 minutes or more during each classroom day	16	28	55	51	23	26	29	3	20	18	20
Cocurricular program separate from regularly graded courses, but occurring during the school day, designed to provide students with the opportunity to pursue leadership roles, special interests, and socialization	16	38	46	40	39	21	27	4	17	15	37
Intramural activities offered for all students during or immediately after the regular classroom day	10	32	58	31	33	36	40	4	17	11	28

Importance of Characteristic:
1 – Little or no importance
2 – Somewhat important
3 – Very important

Current Implementation:
1 – No implementation
2 – Partial implementation
3 – Full implementation

Plans for Implementation:
1 – Implement the characteristic fully and plan to continue to do so
2 – Implement characteristic fully but plan to discontinue in next two years
3 – Do not implement fully but plan to do so in next two years
4 – Do not implement fully but are considering full implementation in the next two years
5 – Do not implement characteristic fully and plan to continue as we are

TABLE 4.16

Opinions About Ability Grouping—Principals, Assistant Principals, and Leadership Team Members

	Principals	Assistant Principals	Leadership Team Members
There should be no form of ability grouping	13	10	7
Ability grouping of students into certain classes as appropriate	64	61	72
Ability grouping of students into any class is not appropriate, but grouping of students for instruction within a class is appropriate.	23	29	21

Leadership team members were most in favor of ability grouping (72 percent) and least in favor of eliminating it (7 percent). If one can assume that leadership team members are mostly teachers, it is reasonable to conclude from this study that teachers still strongly support ability grouping. Thirteen percent of the principals favored no ability grouping, up 5 percent from the 1981 study. Sixty-one percent of the assistant principals favored the practice (lowest percentage of the three groups), and 29 percent approved ability grouping of students into any class (highest percentage of the three groups).

When these data were examined by grade level organization, a majority of the principals in all configurations, with the exception of 5–6–7–8 schools, favored ability grouping (Table 4.17). Two-thirds of 7–8–9, 7–8, and 6–7–8 grade principals favored grouping in certain classes. On the other hand, 53 percent of the 5–6–7–8 principals believed that there should be no ability grouping, or at least no ability grouping across all classes.

TABLE 4.17

Principal Opinions About Ability Grouping—Comparisons by Grade Level Organization of Principal's Current School

	Total	Grade Level Organization				
		7-8-9	7-8	6-7-8	5-6-7-8	Other
There should be no form of ability grouping	13	14	10	10	26	25
Ability grouping of students into certain classes as appropriate	64	69	67	66	47	63
Ability grouping into any class is not appropriate by grouping of students for instruction within a class is appropriate	23	17	23	24	27	12

Issues and Trends

❏ Individualized Promotion

Most middle level schools promote students on an annual basis. Some schools with individualized programs, such as mastery learning, performance-based instruction, or continuous progress curricula, promote students individually based upon the demonstration of mastery. In this study, 16 percent of the administrators reported incidence of individualized promotion rather than grade placement or year-end promotion (Table 4.18). This represents an increase of 7 percentage points over the 1981 study, when only 9 percent of the principals reported using individualized promotion.

TABLE 4.18

Individualized Promotion of Students

Individualized Promotion	Total	Grade Level Organization				
		7-8-9	7-8	6-7-8	5-6-7-8	Other
Yes	16	20	16	14	18	8
No	67	63	64	71	75	62
No, but would like to move in this direction	17	17	20	15	7	30

Seventeen percent of the respondents in this study indicated they would like to move in the direction of individualized promotion. Although not directly comparable, 56 percent of the principals in 1981 reported they were "in favor of some system of individualized promotion for students rather than the customary use of grade placement and year end promotion" (Valentine et al., 1981, p. 85).

Sixty-eight percent of the respondents reported no individualized promotion in their schools. Schools with the 7–8–9 grade level organization had the highest percentage of individualized promotion (20 percent) and the lowest percentage of grade level/year-end promotion (63 percent). Principals of 6–7–8 schools reported the lowest percentage of individualized promotion (14 percent); those in 5–6–7–8 schools indicated the highest percentage of grade level/year-end promotions (75 percent).

❏ Interscholastic Sports

Interscholastic sports continue to be popular in middle level schools. Even at the fifth grade level, more than half the middle level principals surveyed believed that opportunities for participation should be made available (Table 4.19). Compared with the findings of the 1981 study, very few differences were found.

TABLE 4.19

Principal Opinions About Whether or Not Interscholastic Sports Should Be Provided at the Middle Level

	Grade 5		Grade 6		Grade 7		Grade 8		Grade 9	
	'92	'81	'92	'81	'92	'81	'92	'81	'92	'81
Yes	54	58	55	58	78	76	82	84	97	95
No	46	42	45	42	22	24	18	16	3	5

When asked to identify which sports were most appropriate for boys and girls in fifth and sixth grades, principals most frequently marked basketball, gymnastics, soccer, swimming, track, and volleyball. Softball was also identified for fifth and sixth grade girls (Table 4.20).

TABLE 4.20

Principal Opinions About What Interscholastic Sports Should Be Provided at the Middle Level

	Grade 5		Grade 6		Grade 7		Grade 8		Grade 9	
	Boys	Girls	Boys	Girls	Boys	Girls	Boys	Girls	Boys	Girls
No interscholastic sports	46	46	45	45	22	22	18	18	3	3
Baseball	8	5	14	8	31	14	34	15	46	18
Basketball	12	12	28	28	65	65	71	71	59	57
Football	3	3	8	4	36	8	46	10	53	12
Gymnastics	9	9	16	17	29	35	32	38	33	38
Ice Hockey	3	2	5	3	9	5	10	6	20	10
Soccer	12	11	24	23	46	44	51	50	50	47
Softball	6	9	14	21	25	42	27	48	27	50
Swimming	10	10	19	18	35	35	39	39	42	42
Tennis	7	7	16	16	34	34	40	40	49	49
Track	14	14	28	28	62	62	67	67	58	57
Volleyball	8	9	20	24	39	56	42	62	39	56
Wrestling	4	1	12	3	36	6	42	8	47	12
Other	2	3	4	4	7	10	8	10	9	12

For grades 7 through 9 basketball, track, soccer, volleyball, and swimming were frequently identified for both boys and girls. Gymnastics and softball were also cited for girls, and football was cited for boys.

❑ Intramural Sports

Forty-three percent of the principals, 42 percent of the assistant principals, and 37 percent of the leadership team members believed that intramural sports should be emphasized more than interscholastic sports at all grades in the middle level school (Table 4.21). The percentage of principals favoring emphasis of intramural sports over interscholastic sports at all grade levels in the 1992 study was 18 percent higher than in the 1981 study, suggesting a trend to offer more intramural sports activities. This increased emphasis on intramurals appears to have had little effect, however, on the importance assigned interscholastic sports by most middle level educators.

TABLE 4.21

Opinions About Grade Levels Where Greater Emphasis Should Be Placed on Intramural Rather than Interscholastic Activities—Comparison of Principals, Assistant Principals, and Leadership Team Members

Emphasis	Principals	Assistant Principals	Leadership Team Members
All middle level grades	43	42	37
Grades 8 and below	18	14	12
Grades 7 and below	16	14	14
Grades 6 and below	22	27	32
Grade 5	1	3	6

❑ Educational Technology

When asked whether they believed educational technology had improved the quality of learning experiences, 92 percent of the principals, 88 percent of the assistant principals, and 86 percent of the leadership team members said "Yes." Virtually all respondents also believed that educational technology would continue to improve the quality of instruction for future students (98 percent of the principals, 96 percent of the assistant principals, and 95 percent of the leadership team members). Only 70 percent of the principals in the 1981 study believed that technology held promise for improving the quality of their schools.

Computer-assisted instruction (87 percent), educational television channels/programs (63 percent), and computer-managed instruction (49 percent) were the three most frequently cited uses of educational technology in middle level schools (Table 4.22). Only 3 percent of the principals said that no educational technology was employed in their schools.

TABLE 4.22

Types of Educational Technology Used in Middle Level Schools

Educational technology	Total
No educational technology	3
Computer-assisted instruction	87
Educational television channels/programs only	63
Computer-managed instruction	49
Interactive video (within school)	39
Distance education (remote access combining several technologies)	19
Interactive video (remote access)	19
Other	3

Personnel Issues

❏ Preparing Middle Level Teachers

With only 11 percent of the teachers in the sampled schools holding middle level certification, it is evident that many teachers have received little specific preparation for teaching early adolescents. This was confirmed by 44 percent of the principals in this study and 41 percent in the 1981 study. It is not surprising, therefore, that staff development was the most frequently mentioned procedure for preparing middle level teachers in both the 1992 and 1981 studies (Table 4.23).

TABLE 4.23

Procedures Used for Preparing Teachers at Middle Level Schools

Preparation	1992	1981
Inservice programs	73	72
Generally, the staff has had no special preparation to teach at the middle level	44	41
Courses at the university that focus on middle level education	36	44
Student/Practice teaching at the middle level	32	58
Personal study	31	28
Other	2	—

What is surprising, however, is the significant drop since the 1981 study in the mention of university courses on middle level education and student/practice teaching at a middle level school. The incidence of university courses dropped by 8 percentage points, and student/practice teaching fell by 26 points. It would appear that, in spite of the considerable rhetoric about enhancing middle level preparation in college and university teacher education programs, principals perceive these preparation programs as having a significantly lower impact than they did a decade ago.

❏ Excellence in Teaching

Principals, assistant principals, and leadership team members were asked to rank 11 skills and characteristics of excellent middle level teachers. All three groups ranked "competence in adjusting instruction to the varying skills of the students" first, and "competence in developing positive relationships with students in the classroom" second (Table 4.24). There was also agreement at the bottom of the rankings, with all respondents agreeing on "competence in employee behaviors and work habits" (eighth), "competence in working with colleagues" (ninth), "competence in working with parents" (tenth), and "competence in counseling students" (eleventh).

TABLE 4.24

Opinions About Skills and Characteristics of Excellent Middle Level Teachers—Comparisons of Principals, Assistant Principals, and Leadership Team Members (Rankings and Percentages of Response)

Skills/Characteristics	Principals	Assistant Principals	Leadership Team Members
Competence in adjusting instruction to the varying skills of the students	1 (64%)	1 (75%)	1 (69%)
Competence in developing positive relationship with students in the classroom	2 (60%)	2 (58%)	2 (62%)
Competence in use of varied developmentally appropriate methods of instruction	3 (48%)	5 (26%)	5 (34%)
Competence in promoting student self-concept	4 (44%)	3 (41%)	4 (43%)
Competence in subject matter knowledge	5 (29%)	4 (35%)	3 (45%)
Competence in working as a team member	6 (20%)	7 (19%)	7 (17%)
Competence in using positive methods of student discipline	7 (19%)	6 (25%)	6 (18%)
Competence in employee behaviors and work habits (dependability, punctuality, attendance)	8 (5%)	8 (6%)	8 (4%)
Competence in working with colleagues	9 (4%)	9 (4%)	9 (3%)
Competence in working with parents	10 (2%)	10 (3%)	10 (2%)
Competence in counseling students	11 (1%)	11 (1%)	11 (1%)

Some minor differences emerged among the three groups in the intermediate ranking of skills and characteristics. Principals ranked "competence in use of varied and developmentally appropriate methods of instruction" as third, while assistant principals and leadership team members ranked it fifth. Leadership team members ranked "competence in subject matter knowledge" third; principals ranked it fifth; and assistant principals, fourth.

In the 1981 study, principals were given a listing of 10 professional characteristics of teachers and asked to rate them as "not important," "important," or "very important." Because current principals were not asked to rank these characteristics (and some of the wording is different), it is difficult to draw direct comparisons. If, however, characteristics from the 1981 study are ranked by percentages of principals who rated them as important and very important, a few comparisons can be drawn.

"Use positive methods of classroom control" received the highest percentage of important to very important ratings in 1981. "Competence in using positive methods of student discipline" was ranked seventh by principals in 1992. "Employ varied learning strategies" received the second highest percentage in 1981, and "competence in use of varied and developmentally appropriate methods of instruction" was ranked third in 1992. Finally, "counsel students" received the fifth highest percentage in the earlier study, but "competence in counseling students" was ranked dead last (eleventh) by principals in this study.

❑ Collective Bargaining

Twenty-five percent of the principals in this sample reported no collective bargaining in their school districts. As might be expected, there were no collective bargaining agreements exclusively for principals. Principals were included in bargaining agreements with all employees in 31 percent of the schools (Table 4.25).

TABLE 4.25

Principal Opinions About the Status of Collective Bargaining

Status	Total
No collective bargaining	25
Collective bargaining with teachers only	39
Collective bargaining with administrators only	0
Collective bargaining with teachers and administrators	5
Collective bargaining with all employees	31

When asked about the impact of collective bargaining on their schools, 31 percent of the principals indicated it had no appreciable effect on relationships with teachers or on ability to provide educational programs designed specifically for middle level students (Table 4.26). A smaller percentage of principals reported that collective bargaining caused relationships with teachers to deteriorate (14 percent) and lessened ability to provide educational programs designed for middle level students (22 percent).

TABLE 4.26

Principal Opinions About the Impact of Collective Bargaining

Impact *	Total
No collective bargaining	25
Enhanced relationships with teachers	2
No appreciable effect on relationships with teachers	31
Caused relationships with teachers to deteriorate	14
Enhanced ability to provide educational programs specifically designed for middle level students	3
No appreciable effect on ability to provide education programs designed specifically for middle level students	31
Lessened ability to provide educational programs designed for middle level students	22

* More than one response could be selected.

❏ Professional Association Memberships

A high percentage of principals hold memberships in a professional administrator association or union (90 percent) and a "general professional association for the middle level" (66 percent). Principals also hold memberships in honorary professional associations (41 percent). Seventy-one percent of the assistant principals belong to a professional administrator association or union, but they hold significantly fewer memberships in other associations (Table 4.27).

TABLE 4.27

Professional Association Memberships—Principals, Assistant Principals, and Leadership Team Members

Memberships	Principals	Assistant Principals	Leadership Team Members
Professional teacher association or union (e.g., NEA, AFT)	20	24	82
Professional administrator association or union (e.g., NASSP, NAESP)	90	71	10
Subject area professional association (e.g., National Council of Teachers of English)	11	13	56
Honorary professional association (e.g., Phi Delta Kappa)	41	26	20
General professional association for the middle level (e.g., National Middle School Association)	66	36	23
Other	25	17	10
Do not hold membership in a professional association	1	6	2

A majority of the leadership team members are members of a professional teacher association or union (82 percent) and/or a subject area professional association (56 percent). There appeared to be little cross-over of administrators to teacher associations or leadership team member (teacher) memberships to administrator associations. Notable also was the relatively low membership of leadership team members (23 percent) and assistant principals (36 percent) in middle level education associations such as the National Middle School Association.

Eighty percent of the principals, 75 percent of the assistant principals, and 73 percent of the leadership team members reported that their school districts encouraged active participation in professional organizations (Table 4.28). A majority of all three groups also said their districts allowed released time to attend conferences or professional meetings. It should be noted, however, that higher percentages of principals (80 percent) reported released time for conference attendance than assistant principals (64 percent) or leadership team members (59 percent). In addition, principals were more likely to have their membership dues paid by the district, and to have most or all of the expenses for a conference/meeting reimbursed.

94

TABLE 4.28

District Support of Principal, Assistant Principal, and Leadership Team Participation in Professional Associations

The School District:	Principals	Assistant Principals	Leadership Team Members
Discourages active participation in professional organizations	3	1	4
Encourages active participation in professional organizations	80	75	73
Pays my membership dues	51	34	4
Allows released time to attend meetings/ conferences	80	64	59
Pays a portion (half or less) of my expenses to attend meetings/conferences	26	20	23
Pays all or most of my expenses to attend meetings/conferences	53	45	30

❑ Professional Development

A majority of principals reported voluntary participation in six types of professional development activities (Table 4.29), including district activities (74 percent), state professional organization activities (73 percent), state department or regional education agency activities (59 percent), activities conducted by private consultants at an out-of-district location (56 percent), and national professional organization institutes or conferences (53 percent).

Professional development activities in which a majority of the leadership team members voluntarily participated included: district activities (68 percent), state professional organization activities (61 percent), activities conducted by private consultants at an out-of-district location (53 percent), and enrollment in graduate classes at a college or university (52 percent). Voluntary participation of a majority of assistant principals in professional development activities involved only two areas, state professional organization activities (53 percent), and district activities (52 percent). Generally, assistant principals evidenced the lowest participation in professional development activities of the three groups in the study.

Outreach Issues

❑ Articulation with Elementary and High Schools

Middle level schools, because of the position they hold in the educational process, must establish good articulation with both elementary and high schools (Table 4.30).

Articulation issues with elementary schools cited by a majority of principals as "minor" or "major" problems were:

TABLE 4.29

Principal, Assistant Principal, and Leadership Team Member Involvement in Professional Development

Professional Development	Principals	Assistant Principals	Leadership Team Members
National professional organization institute or conference (voluntary participation)	53	30	38
State professional organization institute or conference (voluntary participation)	73	53	61
Activity conducted by private consultants at an out-of-district location (voluntary participation)	56	38	53
District activity required as part of employment	75	67	71
Other district activities (voluntary participation)	74	52	68
Enrollment in graduate courses at a college or university	34	38	52
State department or regional educational agency activity (voluntary participation)	59	32	37
State department or regional education agency activity (required participation)	24	15	11
Principal center or Academy (voluntary participation)	36	22	7
Other	3	2	4

- Teaching methodology (57 percent)
- Instructional delivery systems (56 percent)
- Subject content and sequence (55 percent)
- Student grading practices (51 percent).

A majority of middle level principals also identified the following as problems in articulation with high schools:

- Teaching methodology (63 percent)
- Subject content and sequence (62 percent)
- Instructional delivery systems (56 percent).

With the exception of grading practices, the same articulation problems were experienced with both elementary and high schools. The highest percentages for all problem areas fell into the "minor" response category. Indeed, the majority of the principals reported no articulation problems in seven of the areas at the high school level, and none in eight of the areas at the elementary level.

Coordination of subject content and sequence at both elementary and high school levels was the major articulation problem identified in the 1981 study, and still ranks first or second in the current study.

TABLE 4.30

Articulation Problems as Identified by Middle Level Principals

	Elementary Level 1992			Secondary Level			1981 Study	
	None	Minor	Major	None	Minor	Major	Elem.	Second.
Orientation of students	60	37	3	51	39	10	—	—
Student grading practices	49	43	8	55	39	6	34	22
Instructional delivery systems	44	43	8	55	39	6	—	—
Teaching methodology	43	47	10	37	47	16	—	—
Subject content and sequence	45	45	10	38	52	10	48	49
Pupil promotion policies	57	31	12	57	36	7	33	35
Student records	77	18	5	82	16	2	25	22
Granting subject credit	90	8	2	80	18	2	11	24
Counseling services	57	29	14	62	30	8	37	30
Cocurricular activities	74	22	4	72	25	3	—	—
Interscholastic sports	84	11	5	74	22	4	—	—

❑ Parent Involvement

Forty-eight percent of the respondents indicated that the desire of parents to participate in schools was increasing over previous years (Table 4.31). This represented a significant gain of 18 percentage points over the 1981 study. In 1981, principals had reported a 19 percent decrease in the desire of parents to be involved, so the impetus seems to have reversed. Parents are more likely to be involved in today's middle level schools. Principals of 6–7–8 schools reported the highest percentage of increased parental participation (57 percent), while principals of 5–6–7–8 schools indicated the greatest decrease.

TABLE 4.31

Principal Opinions About Parental Desire To Participate in Middle Level Schools—Comparison to 1981 Study and By Grade Level Organization

	Totals		1992				
Parental Participation	1992	1981	7–8–9	7–8	6–7–8	5–6–7–8	Other
Increasing over previous years	48	30	33	41	57	33	33
Decreasing over previous years	11	19	10	9	10	14	33
About the same as previous years	41	52	57	50	33	53	33

❏ Community Involvement

A majority of the principals said the desire of community members to participate in middle level schools had remained about the same as in previous years (Table 4.32). Principals of 6–7–8 schools reported the highest increase in the desire for participation (37 percent), while 5–6–7–8 schools showed the largest decrease (21 percent).

TABLE 4.32						
Principal Opinions About Community Members' Desire To Participate in Middle Level Schools—Comparisons by Grade Level Organization						
Community Participation	Total	7–8–9	7–8	6–7–8	5–6–7–8	Other
Increasing over previous years	32	31	29	37	27	20
Decreasing from previous years	15	15	20	12	21	20
About the same as previous years	53	54	51	51	42	60

❏ Special Interest Groups

Principals were given a list of 15 community groups or organizations (Table 4.33) and asked to assess the influence each group had exerted on their school in the past two years. Six groups were identified by a majority of the principals as having "moderate influence" or "extreme influence."

- PTA or PTO (72 percent)
- Teachers' association or union (65 percent)
- Local high schools (63 percent)
- Local elementary schools (58 percent)
- Citizenship or parent groups—non-PTA (55 percent)
- The business community (54 percent).

Groups having the least or no influence included: "extreme left-wing individuals/groups" (96 percent), "extreme right-wing individuals/groups" (92 percent), "censorship groups—books, programs, etc." (86 percent), and "women's rights or minority organizations" (85 percent). Issues such as censorship and pressures from right/left-wing groups attract the attention of the media, but they were perceived by principals as having very little influence on middle level schools.

These findings are similar to those of the 1981 NASSP study, when principals identified local elementary and high schools, teachers' associations/unions, and PTAs/PTOs as having the greatest influence. Groups having the least influence then were right/left-wing groups, local labor organizations, legal aid groups, and censorship groups.

TABLE 4.33

Principal Opinions About the Influence of Special Interest Groups

Interest Group	Little/No Influence	Moderate Influence	Extreme Influence
Censorship groups (books, programs, etc.)	86	13	1
Citizenship or parent groups (non-PTA)	45	44	11
Extreme left-wing individuals/groups	96	3	1
Extreme right-wing individuals/groups	92	6	2
Individuals/groups concerned about national reports/studies	69	30	1
Legal aid groups	90	9	1
Local elementary schools	42	52	6
Local high schools	37	54	9
Local media (editorial policy)	58	29	3
PTA or PTO	28	52	20
Religious or church organization	78	20	2
State colleges and/or universities	72	28	1
Teachers' association or union	35	42	23
The business community	46	49	5
Women's rights or minority organizations	85	13	2
Other (e.g., local advisory committee, taxpayers organization, state department)	69	9	22

Summary

Principals, assistant principals, and leadership team members reported that the most important tasks of American schools were helping students acquire basic skills, develop positive self-concept and good human relations, develop skills in critical thinking and problem solving, and prepare for a changing world. These same four tasks were ranked in this same order by high school principals in the 1988 NASSP High School Study. Middle level principals also ranked the top three items the same in the 1981 NASSP study, but placed "preparation for a changing world" in sixth place.

The 6–7–8 grade level organization was identified as the "ideal" structure by almost three-fourths of the principals in this study. The preference for the 6–7–8 grade level organization has increased since 1981, when 53 percent of the principals selected it as "the ideal" configuration.

Sixty-five percent of the principals reported they had changed their schools to a 5–6–7–8 or 6–7–8 grade level organization, a much higher percentage than was reported in the 1981 study (35 percent). The primary reasons for making the change were to provide a program best suited to the needs of the middle level student, to provide a better transition from elementary to high school, and to employ new curriculum and instructional innovations. Only one-third of the principals reported that the grade levels of their schools were changed to adjust for enrollment trends, so it would appear that middle level schools are being used less frequently to solve enrollment problems at high schools and elementary schools.

Two-thirds of the principals in this study indicated the optimal enrollment for a middle level school was in the 400–799 range. This range was supported by a majority of all principals, regardless of the grade level organization of their own school.

Dramatic changes have taken place in the use of technology for administrative purposes since the 1981 study, when 42 percent of the principals said they did not even have access to information processing equipment. Eighty-eight percent of the principals in this study used some form of technology for administrative purposes.

Middle level principals indicated a strong preference for school policy leadership based upon best professional judgment, and sharing decision making with faculty members on important issues. Only about a third of the respondents felt that they should "primarily represent the interest of parents, leaders, and patrons of the school."

A majority of the principals identified 17 factors as either "moderate" or "extreme" roadblocks to doing an effective job. Fourteen roadblocks were cited by a majority of assistant principals and leadership team members. Five factors topped the lists of all three groups: inability to obtain funding, lack of time for myself, resistance to change, variations in the ability and dedication of the staff, and parents apathetic and irresponsible about their children.

> Principals, assistant principals, and leadership team members all ranked "competence in adjusting instruction to the varying skills of the students" and "competence in developing positive relationships with students in the classroom" as the two most important skills or characteristics of middle level teachers.

Three-fourths of the principals, assistant principals, and leadership team members indicated that interdisciplinary teaming was very important. Exploratory programs were also rated as important by all three groups. A majority of principals believed that adviser/advisee programs were very important, but fewer than half the assistant principals and leadership team members agreed. High levels of support also emerged for cocurricular programs and intramural activities. Considerable enthusiasm was reported for these five characteristics/programs, but, with the exception of exploratory programs, they were being fully implemented in fewer than 40 percent of the schools.

Ability grouping in middle level schools was supported by a majority of principals, assistant principals, and leadership team members. The type of grouping favored by all three groups was "ability grouping of students into certain classes as appropriate."

Most middle level schools in this study promote students on an annual basis, but a small number of principals (16 percent) reported using individualized promotion. This represents an increase over the 1981 NASSP study.

Interscholastic sports continued to attract about the same level of support as in the 1981 study. A majority of principals believed that interscholastic sports should be available to fifth graders, but the level of support increases to 97 percent at the ninth grade. The sports identified as most appropriate for fifth and sixth graders were basketball, gymnastics, soccer, swimming, track, and volleyball. For grades 7 through 9, basketball, track, soccer, volleyball, and swimming were most frequently listed. Softball and gymnastics were also identified for girls and football for boys.

Compared to the 1981 study, there was considerably more support in this study for emphasis on intramural sports over interscholastic sports at all middle level grades. This trend, however, appeared to have little impact on the actual value ascribed to interscholastic sports by most middle level educators.

Most respondents reported that educational technology had improved the quality of learning experiences in their schools, and that it will continue to do so for future students. Most frequently identified uses of educational technology were computer-assisted instruction, educational television, and computer-managed instruction.

Forty-four percent of the principals in this study indicated that their teachers had no special preparation for teaching in middle level schools. Staff development remained the primary means of middle level teacher preparation. Of significance was the considerable drop since 1981 in the number of teachers taking middle level university courses and student teaching in middle level schools.

Principals, assistant principals, and leadership team members all ranked "competence in adjusting instruction to the varying skills of the students" and "competence in developing positive relationships with students in the classroom" as the two most important skills or characteristics of middle level teachers. Also ranked in the upper half by all three groups were "competence in the use of varied and developmentally appropriate methods of instruction," "competence in promoting student self-concept," and "competence in subject matter knowledge."

No collective bargaining agreements existed in one-fourth of the schools in this study. Thirty-nine percent of the principals reported collective bargaining for teachers only, and 31 percent indicated arrangements for all employees. No agreements for administrators alone were reported. Almost a third of the respondents said that collective bargaining had no appreciable effect on relationships with teachers, or on providing specifically designed middle level programs. Fewer than 25 percent cited any deleterious effects of collective bargaining.

A majority of principals and assistant principals reported memberships in professional administrator associations, and a majority of leadership team members held memberships in teacher professional associations or unions and subject area professional associations. A majority of principals also had memberships in general middle level professional associations. Principals, assistant principals, and leadership team members indicated high levels of district support for participation in professional associations. A majority of all three groups reported they received released time to participate in conferences and professional meetings.

More than half the principals reported voluntary involvement in various professional develop-ment activities. Leadership team members also indicated a high level of voluntary involvement, but assistant principal involvement was much lower.

A majority of principals identified three common articulation problems with both elementary and high schools: in teaching methodology, subject content and sequence, and instructional deliv-ery systems.

The desire for parents to become involved in schools was reported as increasing by almost half the principals. This represented a significant gain over the 1981 study. Some principals said the desire of community members to participate had increased over previous years, but a majority indicated it had remained about the same.

Special interest groups or organizations experiencing the most success in influencing middle level schools were PTAs or PTOs, teacher associations or unions, local high schools and elemen-tary schools, citizenship or parent groups (non-PTA), and the business community. Those identi-fied as exerting little or no influence were extreme right/left wing groups, censorship groups, and women's rights or minority organizations. These findings were very similar to those of the 1981 NASSP study.

Chapter 5

Leadership Profiles

Middle level education came of age during the 1980s. To be sure, much maturing is still ahead, but the difficult developmental steps have been taken that can ensure a rewarding maturity. The divisive arguments about middle school vs. junior high school are largely a thing of the past. Middle level education has achieved an identity that represents a pattern of grades from 5 to 9, and that emphasizes student growth and development.

As the research team planned this study, the following questions guided the deliberations.

1. Are there differences in the preparation and beliefs of middle level principals, assistant principals, and members of school leadership teams?

2. Is the leadership of today's middle level schools different from 1981 and 1966?

3. Has the concept of a "leadership team" emerged in middle level schools?

4. What are the beliefs of middle level educators about specific educational programs, and are the programs in middle level schools congruent with those beliefs?

5. Are the programs in today's middle level schools different from those reported in previous studies?

6. What practices are used in schools experiencing successful restructuring of their middle level programs? (Phase 2 only.)

This study investigated these questions in terms of the personal, professional, and organizational characteristics of leaders and schools, school leadership issues, educational program trends, and leader views on middle level issues and trends. The most significant findings are reported here under those headings.

Personal/Professional/
Organizational Characteristics

Only one personal characteristic emerged as significant in this study. During a decade when the number of female principals at the elementary and high school levels remained fairly constant at 21 percent and 11 percent respectively, the middle level experienced a significant surge. The number of female principals at the middle level increased by 15 percent, to 21 percent in 1992. Females also constituted more than one-third of all assistant principals in middle level schools, and two-thirds of all leadership team members.

Several professional characteristics were noteworthy.

■ An increasing number of today's middle level principals have come to the principalship from the middle level assistant principalship. This is an increase of 7 percent since 1981, and a striking 16 percent since 1966. If the additional 9 percent promoted directly from middle level teaching is considered, 45 percent of middle level principals come directly from another position in a middle level school. The middle level is creating its own corps of leadership.

■ Virtually all middle level principals and assistant principals, and two-thirds of leadership team members, hold the master's degree or above. Twenty percent of all principals have completed the coursework for, or earned, the doctorate. Females are better prepared than their male counterparts.

> Principals, assistant principals, and leadership team members all ranked "competence in adjusting instruction to the varying skills of the students" and "competence in developing positive relationships with students in the classroom" as the two must important skills or characteristics of middle level teachers

More than half the female middle level principals have earned the specialist (six year) or doctoral degree, contrasted with fewer than one-third of the males. This trend has widened by 10 points since 1981.

■ Fifty percent of current middle level principals plan to remain in their present positions for three to five years. This resolve is an increase of 13 percent over 1981, but approximately the same as 1966. Many 1981 respondents functioned during the difficult years of the 1960s and 1970s, and were understandably considering a change. Sixty-two percent of responding leadership team members will also remain in their present positions for three to five years. Twenty-two percent are interested in the middle level principalship, an encouraging finding for the next generation of leadership. A disturbing trend since 1966 is the drop in percentage of middle level principals interested in the superintendency or the professorship. Interest in the superintendency dropped a jolting 20 percent since 1981, and fewer than 1 percent of the current respondents contemplated a move to a college or university position (8 percent in 1966). An embattled superintendency likely accounts for the former, and salary differentials for the latter.

- Two school organizational trends merit mention. Principals reported that average daily attendance has increased a commendable 11 percent since 1981. Surely, some of that improvement can be traced to the more client-centered environment resulting from implementation of middle level philosophy, programs, and grade patterns.

- Grade organizational patterns have almost reversed since 1966. Traditional junior high-type 7–8–9 configurations declined from 67 percent in 1966 to a current 15 percent. The distribution of 6–7–8 schools increased from 5 percent in 1966 to 50 percent in 1992. The percentage of 5–6–7–8 schools also increased by eight points since 1981, probably reflecting the current thinking of some middle level scholars and practitioners.

School Leadership Issues

The 1980s saw an increasing public policy emphasis on educational restructuring, with emergence of collaborative initiatives such as site-based management, shared governance, and teacher empowerment. NASSP national survey findings on school leadership were interesting but not highly supportive of greater levels of collaborative decision making in middle level schools. Significant findings included the following.

- Sixty-eight percent of responding principals reported leadership teams in their schools. Principals and other staff members did not agree on the composition of teams, suggesting that team membership may, in fact, not be well-defined in many schools.

- Assistant principals were reported serving in 77 percent of the schools. Forty-three percent of the schools had female assistants.

- Eighty-six percent of all middle level teaching staff members were female. This shift, up from 62 percent in 1981, resembles elementary school staffing patterns and could mean trouble for boys needing male role models during these difficult developmental years.

- Certification of middle level teachers remains primarily secondary, although middle level certification is more widely available. Incidence of secondary certification declined significantly among middle level teachers since 1981 (from 80 to 63 percent), and elementary certification increased by a similar percentage. This certification trend is a positive one since, lacking substantial numbers of middle-certificated staff, a mix of elementary and secondary-trained teachers better meets the needs of developing adolescents.

- The number of reported hours that building leaders work is up dramatically since 1981. Eighty-eight percent of the principals reported working an average of 50 hours or more in a typical week. Twice as many as in 1981 worked 60–69 hours, and three times as many reported 70 hours or more.

- Assistant principals perceived their primary role as working with students on behavior, a rather traditional picture of life as an assistant. They also spent time on student activities and the day-to-day management of the school. They viewed program development and personnel work as high priorities, but spent their time in traditional roles. Apparently, assistant principals have not yet emerged as significant educational leaders in the restructuring of middle level schools.

- The most important instructional leadership duties of assistant principals and leadership team members were scheduling, curriculum, instructional improvement, school goal setting, and staff development. Team members also reported other primary responsibilities in department teams, adviser/advisee programs, and interdisciplinary teams.

- Generally, the 1992 findings do not reflect a high degree of staff involvement in decision making. Leadership team members and staff committees were typically involved only in discussion or in making recommendations, rather than in reaching actual decisions. The degree of change in staff-shared decision making since 1981 is modest at best.

- Principals experienced somewhat greater personal participation in determining school budget allocations since 1981. They also reported notably more authority for general staffing decisions (up 31 percent since 1966), but less freedom to make alternative personnel decisions such as employing aides rather than teachers.

- Middle level leaders are well satisfied on the majority of basic job issues. All respondent groups were most satisfied by their rapport with students and teachers, and least satisfied with the time they had to devote to the job, and with their salaries.

Educational Program Trends

The contemporary movement for school restructuring emphasizes organizational and program reforms orchestrated systemwide to involve all affected levels of school operation and authority. Ultimately, the results of restructuring must become apparent in the individual school. The study investigated several organizational structures that affect middle level programs to assess whether any currently recommended changes in school operation have actually taken place. These were the most notable findings.

- Fifty-seven percent of all schools surveyed used an interdisciplinary team organization. Schools with grades 6–8 and 5–8 employed teaming the most, 7–9 schools the least. Teaming was almost nonexistent in the ninth grade.

- Team membership was most often determined by school administrators, with or without teacher input. Team leaders were utilized in 77 percent of the teaming schools, most often selected by the teams. Fifty-four percent of the teaming schools reported a common plus on individual teacher planning period. More than one-third reported that all members of the team had one common planning period.

- Ability grouping is still widely used in middle level schools (82 percent). Schools with grades 7–8 and 7–9 more often grouped by ability. The current study revealed a slight decrease (6 percent) in this practice across all grade level organizations, with the exception of 7–8–9 schools. Schools with a sixth grade tended to group by ability the least.

- Specialized forms of ability grouping for the gifted and talented continue to increase. Fourteen percent more middle level schools now offer these programs than in 1981.

■ Instructional format varied little by subject area, but notably by grade level. Self-contained classrooms predominated at the fifth grade. Interdisciplinary teaming was most prevalent in the sixth grade. Period-by-period or departmentalized organization dominated the seventh, eighth, and ninth grades.

■ The variety of required and elective courses offered in most middle level schools reconfirmed the presence of a broad-based curriculum, with curricular integration an increasingly higher priority where interdisciplinary teaming predominated.

Leader Views on Issues and Trends

Documenting administrator views on current issues and trends constituted a major objective of this national study. Some of the most interesting findings were detected in this area.

■ Principals surveyed since 1965 in six NASSP national studies have ranked the acquisition of basic skills as the foremost task of American schools. Principals, assistant principals, and leadership team members in the current study all agreed on the top four tasks: acquisition of basic skills, development of positive self-concept and human relations skills, development of skills in critical inquiry and problem solving, and preparation for a changing world. Development of moral and spiritual values dropped from second in the 1966 study to seventh in the 1992 study.

■ Seventy-two percent of all respondents in this study favored a 6–7–8 grade pattern for middle level schools. Principal support jumped 18 points, from 54 percent in 1981, to 72 percent in 1992.

■ Dramatic increases have occurred in the administrative use of technology since 1981, with 88 percent of the principals reporting use most frequently for maintaining attendance records, preparing grade reports, preparing brochures and newsletters, and scheduling classes.

■ Two-thirds of the principals, assistant principals, and leadership team members identified 5 of 26 listed factors as moderate or extreme roadblocks to effective principal leadership: inability to obtain funding, lack of time for self, resistance to change, variations in staff ability and dedication, and apathetic or irresponsible parents.

■ Survey respondents rated as very important to important five characteristics of instructionally effective middle level schools as defined by current research and best practice. Interdisciplinary teaming topped the list, followed by exploratory course offerings, intramural activities, adviser-advisee programs, and cocurricular programs. Principals reported that exploratory programs had the highest incidence of full implementation in their schools (55 percent), followed by interdisciplinary teaming and intramural activities (36 percent), adviser-advisee programs (26 percent), and cocurricular programs (21 percent).

■ More than half the principals believed that interscholastic sports should be available to all students. Approximately 40 percent of all respondents also said that intramural sports should be emphasized over interscholastic sports, up 18 percent for principals since 1981.

■ Middle level teachers have received little preservice preparation for teaching pre and early adolescents. Inservice programs are the dominant form of staff development. Since 1981, the incidence of university course preparation dropped 8 percentage points, and student/practice teaching in middle level schools fell by 26 points.

■ Parent desire to participate in middle level schools jumped a significant 18 percent since 1981. The 1981 survey had reported a 19 percent drop, so the impetus seems to have reversed. Parents are more likely to be involved today.

Major Findings

Reflecting on the questions that prefaced this report and chapter, a few major findings can be cited for reflection and as a framework for future research.

1. Differences do exist in the preparation of middle level principals, assistant principals, and leadership team members, but, for the most part, they are not very consequential. Almost all principals and assistant principals have earned the master's degree, or better. Two-thirds of leadership team members have attained the same level of preparation. Females are better prepared than males. More than half the female principals hold the doctoral or specialist degree, as contrasted with fewer than one-third of the males. A notable concern is a lack of specific middle level teacher preservice preparation. University coursework and student/practice teaching in middle level schools have dropped sharply (26 percent).

2. The leadership of today's middle level schools has changed since 1981 in two important ways. Some 45 percent of current principals come directly from another position in a middle level school. Even more significant, the number of female principals has increased 15 percent since 1981, to a total of 21 percent in 1992. More than one-third of all current assistant principals and two-thirds of leadership team members are females.

3. Leadership teams are now functioning in 68 percent of middle level schools. Principals and other team members often disagree on the formality of membership, implying that the teams may be quite informal and not well defined. The current findings do not suggest that staff members are highly involved in decision making. Leadership team members and staff committees were most often involved only at the level of discussion or in preparing recommendations, not in making the actual decisions.

4. Respondents strongly supported salient elements of the current middle level model. Principals, assistant principals, and leadership team members all rated as important to very important five characteristics of instructionally effective middle level schools. Interdisciplinary teaming was rated first, followed by exploratory courses, intramural activities, adviser-advisee programs, and cocurricular programs. However, only 55 percent of the schools have fully implemented exploratory programs; 36 percent, interdisciplinary teaming and intramural activities; and fewer than 30 percent, adviser-advisee and cocurricular programs. Rhetoric is still stronger than program in most schools. This is particularly evident in beliefs about intramural and interscholastic sports. More than half the principals believed that interscholastic sports should be available to students, even fifth graders. Yet, about 40 percent said that intramural sports should be emphasized over interscholastic sports.

5. Programs in contemporary middle level schools are generally similar to those reported in earlier NASSP studies. The basic required subjects remained much the same as in 1981. Interesting trends included a small but general decline in schools requiring courses, especially in grades 5 and 6. However, a slight increase was evident for science and social studies courses in grades 7–9. Science is now required in ninth grade 10 percent more often than in 1981. Instrumental music remains the most popular elective in all grades.

6. Most encouraging findings:

- The majority of principals and leadership team members plan to remain in their present positions for three to five years. Schools can expect some stability in leadership.
- Average daily attendance is up by 11 percent since 1981. The client-centered environment recommended by the middle level model surely has been a factor in this improvement.
- Administrators are using technology much more than in 1981, with 88 percent of principals reporting usage particularly for attendance, grade reporting, scheduling, and school communications.
- Parents are more involved in today's schools. Level of participation jumped 18 percent since 1981.

7. Most frustrating findings:

- Career interest among principals in the superintendency or the professorship has dropped disturbingly, casting doubt on the emergence of a talent pool for the next generation of these positions.
- Eighty-six percent of all middle level teachers are now female, raising questions about adequate numbers of male role models for boys during these difficult years of development.
- Assistant principals reported that their primary role expectations and time were centered on working with student behavior, a very traditional view of the position and not indicative of new leadership patterns within the school leadership team.
- Ability grouping is still widely supported and utilized in middle level schools (82 percent). Scholarly consensus opposes both tracking and most forms of ability grouping, but schools showed only a slight decrease (6 percent) in the practice since 1981.

Some Concluding Observations

The following general impressions constitute an overview of the three themes—leadership/personnel, program, and beliefs—that undergird this study.

❏ Leadership/Personnel Trends

- The female presence now dominates middle level schools. The number of well-prepared female principals is rapidly increasing.
- Teachers (and school leaders) have limited middle level preparation.
- Shared leadership/participative management is not yet widely practiced.

- Teaming is increasing both at the school leadership level and for interdisciplinary organization of curriculum and instruction.

❑ Program Trends

- Interdisciplinary teaming, exploratory course offerings, and intramural programs are making inroads; adviser-advisee and cocurricular programs are struggling.
- Integration of knowledge is now often addressed with the increase of interdisciplinary teaming but has yet to be seriously incorporated into most middle level programs.
- Standard scheduling is still pervasive in middle level schools.
- Traditional forms of instructional organization (classroom, departmental) predominate in the fifth and seventh to ninth grades. Interdisciplinary teaming is most prevalent at the sixth grade.

❑ Belief Systems

- Support of ability grouping is still high.
- Controversy about intramural vs. interscholastic sports continues.
- Assistant principals still construe their role in a traditional and narrow fashion.
- The debate about 7–9 vs. 6–8 grade patterns has been settled in favor of the latter, but a trend to include grade 5 is again emerging.

References

Alexander, W.M., and McEwin, C.K. *Schools in the Middle: Status and Progress.* Columbus, Ohio: National Middle School Association, 1989.

————. *Earmarks of Schools in the Middle: A Research Report.* Boone, N.C.: Appalachian State University, 1969.

Alexander, W.M.; Williams, E.I.; Compton, M.; Hines, V.A.; Prescott, D.; and Kealy, R. *The Emergent Middle School.* New York: Holt, Rinehart & Winston, 1968.

Arhar, J.M. *Research in Middle Level Education: Interdisciplinary Team Organization.* Columbus, Ohio: National Middle School Association, 1992.

Beane, J.A. *A Middle School Curriculum: From Rhetoric to Reality.* Columbus, Ohio: National Middle School Association, 1990.

Becker, H.J. "Curriculum and Instruction in Middle Grade Schools." *Phi Delta Kappan* 6(1990): 450–57.

Braddock, J.H., II. "Tracking the Middle Grades: National Patterns of Grouping for Instruction." *Phi Delta Kappan* 6(1990): 445–49.

Brazee, E. "The Tip of the Iceberg or the Edge of the Glacier: Curriculum Development in Middle Schools." *Mainely Middle* (1989): 18–22.

Brooks, K., and Edwards, F. *The Middle School in Transition.* Lexington, Ky.: University of Kentucky, 1978.

Carnegie Council on Adolescent Development. *Turning Points: Preparing American Youth for the 21st Century.* New York: Carnegie Council, 1989.

Clark, S.N., and Clark, D.C. *Restructuring the Middle Level School: Implications for Middle Level Leaders.* Albany, N.Y.: State University of New York Press, in press.

Duttweiler, P.A. *Organizing the Education System for Excellence: Harnessing the Energy of People.* Report No. EA 022 797. Austin, Tex.: Southwest Educational Development Laboratory, 1990. ERIC Document Reproduction Service No. ED 331 121.

Epstein, J.L., and Mac Iver, D.J. *Education in the Middle Grades: National Practices and Trends.* Columbus, Ohio: National Middle School Association, 1990.

Erb, T.O., and Doda, N.M. *Team Organization: Promise, Practices, and Possibilities.* Washington, D.C.: National Education Association, 1989.

George, P.S. "Tracking and Ability Grouping: Which Way the Middle School?" *Middle School Journal* 20(1988): 21–28.

Irvin, J.L. "Developmentally Appropriate Instruction in Middle Level Schools: Results from a U.S. Survey." *Journal of Reading* 32(1992): 306–11.

Irvin, J.L., and Connors, N.A. "Developmentally Appropriate Instruction: The Heart of the Middle School." In *Transforming Middle Level Education: Perspectives and Possibilities,* edited by J.L. Irvin. Boston: Allyn and Bacon, 1989a.

———. "Reading Instruction in Middle Level Schools: Results from a U.S. Survey." *Journal of Reading* 32(1989b): 306–11.

Jenkins, John M. *Advisement Programs: A New Look at an Old Practice.* Reston, Va.: National Association of Secondary School Principals, 1992.

Keefe, J.W. *Learning Style Theory and Practice.* Reston, Va.: National Association of Secondary School Principals, 1987.

Klein, E. "Lamar Alexander: We're Talking About a Revolution." *Parade Magazine,* August 25, 1991.

Lipsitz, Joan. *Successful Schools for Young Adolescents.* New Brunswick, N.J.: Transaction Books, 1984.

Lounsbury, J.H. *As I See It.* Columbus, Ohio: National Middle School Association, 1991.

Lounsbury, J.H., and Clark, D.C. *Inside Grade Eight: From Apathy to Excitement.* Reston, Va.: National Association of Secondary School Principals, 1990.

Mac Iver, D.J. "A National Description of Report Card Entries in the Middle Grades." CBS Report 9. Baltimore, Md.: The Johns Hopkins University Center for Research on Effective Schooling for Disadvantaged Students, 1990.

Merenbloom, E.Y. *The Team Process: Handbook for Teachers,* 3d ed. Columbus, Ohio: National Middle School Association, 1991.

National Association of Secondary School Principals, Council on Middle Level Education. *This We Believe,* 2d ed. Columbus, Ohio: Author, 1985.

Oakes, J. *Keeping Track: How Schools Structure Inequality.* New Haven, Conn.: Yale University Press, 1985.

Rock, D.A., and Hemphill, J.K. *The Junior High-School Principalship.* Reston, Va.: National Association of Secondary School Principals, 1966.

Spear, R.C. "Appropriate Grouping Practices for Middle Level Students." In *Transforming Middle Level Education: Perspectives and Possibilities,* edited by J.L. Irvin. Boston, Mass.: Allyn and Bacon, 1992.

Toepfer, C.F. "Middle Level Curriculum: Defining the Elusive." In *Transforming Middle Level Education: Perspective and Possibilities,* edited by J.L. Irvin. Boston, Mass.: Allyn and Bacon, 1992.

Valentine, J., and Mogar, D.C. "Middle Level Certification, An Encouraging Evolution." *Middle School Journal,* November 1992.

Valentine, J.; Clark, D.C.; Nickerson, N.C., Jr.; and Keefe, J. *The Middle Level Principalship: A Survey of Middle Level Principals and Programs,* Vol. I. Reston, Va.: National Association of Secondary School Principals, 1981.

Vars, G.F. "Humanizing Student Evaluation and Reporting." In *Transforming Middle Level Education: Perspectives and Possibilities,* edited by J.L. Irvin. Boston, Mass.: Allyn and Bacon, 1992.

References

Appendix

❏ A National Study of Leadership in Middle Level
Education—Principal Survey: Form A

❏ A National Study of Leadership in Middle Level
Education—Principal Survey: Form B

❏ A National Study of Leadership in Middle Level
Education—Assistant Principal Survey

❏ A National Study of Leadership in Middle Level
Education—Leadership Team Member Survey

National Association of Secondary School Principals

A National Study of Leadership In Middle Level Education

Principal Survey: Form A

Directions

Your questionnaire is identified by the label placed on it. It is not necessary to sign or place your name on the questionnaire. In reporting results, only statistical summaries of the responses of groups of principals will be cited. In no case will the identity of an individual be divulged. You are urged to make every answer a sincere one.

Circle the number of the appropriate response using pen or pencil. If you change a response, please make the change obvious so there is no doubt about how you wish to answer.

Please attempt to answer every question. For some questions none of the alternatives may correspond exactly to your situation, or to the opinion you hold. In such cases mark the alternative which comes closest to the answer you would like to give.

For the purposes of this study, two terms should be clarified:

(1) **Middle level education** is a general phase used to encompass various combinations of grades five through nine.

(2) **Principal** refers to the chief building administrator and should not be confused with the assistant principal or vice principal.

> The cover letter provided criteria for determining whether the Assistant Principal (blue form) and the Leadership Team (green form) should be distributed in your school. Please indicate below whether you did or did not distribute the two surveys and the job title of the person(s) to whom you gave them.
>
> ☐ I gave the Assistant Principal Survey to: (job title) _____.
> ☐ I did not distribute the Assistant Principal Survey.
> ☐ I gave the Leadership Team Survey to: (job title) _____.
> ☐ I did not distribute the Leadership Team Survey.

Return your completed questionnaire to NASSP in the envelope provided. Thank you for your participation in this important study.

Please Return This Questionnaire Within 10 Days

Advisory Committee for the National Study of Leadership in Middle Level Education:
James Anding, Nathan Hale Junior High School, Omaha, NE; James Aseltine, Irving Robbins Middle School, Farmington, CT; Don Dalton, Canyon Vista Middle School, Austin, TX; Marion Payne, Owen Brown Middle School, Columbia, MD; Lori Simmons, Commodore Bainbridge Middle School, Bainbridge Island, WA; Joseph Tafoya, Santa Ana Unified School District, Santa Ana, CA; Sue Carol Thompson, Blue Valley School District, Overland Park, KS.

Research Team:
Donald Clark, University of Arizona; Judith Irvin, Florida State University; James Keefe, NASSP; George Melton, NASSP Emeritus; Jerry Valentine, University of Missouri

Demographic and Control Questions

1. What is your sex?
   - (1) Male
   - (2) Female

2. What is your age?
   - (1) 24 and under
   - (2) 25-29
   - (3) 30-34
   - (4) 35-39
   - (5) 40-44
   - (6) 45-49
   - (7) 50-54
   - (8) 55-59
   - (9) 60 or older

3. With what ethnic group would you identify yourself?
   - (1) White
   - (2) Black
   - (3) Chicano/Hispanic
   - (4) American Indian
   - (5) Asian
   - (6) Other:_____

4. At what age were you appointed to your first principalship?
   - (1) 24 and under
   - (2) 25-29
   - (3) 30-34
   - (4) 35-39
   - (5) 40-44
   - (6) 45-49
   - (7) 50-54
   - (8) 55-59
   - (9) 60 or older

5. How many total years have you served as a principal of this and other schools, including this current year?
   - (1) One
   - (2) 2-3
   - (3) 4-5
   - (4) 6-7
   - (5) 8-9
   - (6) 10-14
   - (7) 15-19
   - (8) 20-24
   - (9) 25 or more

6. How many years of teaching experience, regardless of level, did you have prior to taking your present position? Do not include years as a full-time administrator or supervisor.
   - (1) None
   - (2) One
   - (3) 2-3
   - (4) 4-6
   - (5) 7-9
   - (6) 10-14
   - (7) 15-19
   - (8) 20-24
   - (9) 25 or more

7. What is the highest degree you have earned?
   - (1) Less than bachelor's
   - (2) Bachelor's degree
   - (3) Master's degree in education
   - (4) Master's degree not in education
   - (5) Master's degree plus some additional graduate work
   - (6) Educational Specialist, six-year program or equivalent
   - (7) Master's degree plus *all coursework* for a doctorate
   - (8) Doctor of Education
   - (9) Doctor of Philosophy
   - (10) Other:_____

8. Which of the following *best* represents your administrative certification for the principalship? *Circle only one answer.*
   - (1) Secondary
   - (2) Middle
   - (3) Elementary
   - (4) No principalship certification
   - (5) Other:_____

9. What was the last position you held prior to becoming a middle level principal? *Circle only one answer.*
   - (1) Elementary teacher
   - (2) Middle level teacher
   - (3) High school teacher
   - (4) Assistant principal of an elementary school
   - (5) Assistant principal of a middle level school
   - (6) Assistant principal of a high school
   - (7) Principal of an elementary school
   - (8) Principal of a high school
   - (9) Guidance counselor
   - (10) Central office administrator
   - (11) College administrator or instructor
   - (12) Other:_____

10. What is your current annual salary? *Do not consider fringe benefits.*
    - (1) Less than $30,000
    - (2) 30,000-34,999
    - (3) 35,000-39,999
    - (4) 40,000-44,999
    - (5) 45,000-49,999
    - (6) 50,000-54,999
    - (7) 55,000-59,999
    - (8) 60,000-64,999
    - (9) 65,000-69,999
    - (10) 70,000 or more
    - (11) Not applicable (religious order)

11. What is the basis for your salary determination?
    - (1) Percentage of a step in the teacher salary schedule
    - (2) Teacher salary schedule plus an increment for administration
    - (3) Negotiations are held for administration separate from teachers
    - (4) Negotiated on an individual basis
    - (5) Non-negotiated administrative salary schedule
    - (6) Does not apply (e.g., religious order)
    - (7) Other:_____

12. Do you have *tenure as a principal?*
    - (1) Yes
    - (2) No

13. Which of the following categories best describes the middle level school of which you are principal. *Select only one.*
    - (1) Public
    - (2) Parochial or diocesan
    - (3) Private, religious affiliated
    - (4) Private, not religious affiliated
    - (5) Other:_____

14. How many students are currently enrolled in your school?
    (1) Less than 200
    (2) 200-399
    (3) 400-599
    (4) 600-799
    (5) 800-999
    (6) 1000-1199
    (7) 1200-1399
    (8) 1400-1599
    (9) 1600-1799
    (10) 1800-1999
    (11) 2000 or more

15. What do you estimate is the percent of average daily attendance of those enrolled in your school *this school year*?
    (1) Less than 50%
    (2) 51-60%
    (3) 61-70%
    (4) 71-80%
    (5) 81-90%
    (6) 91-95%
    (7) 96% or more

16. What was the average per pupil expenditure (exclusive of capital outlay) for each student in your school during the 1990-91 school year?
    (1) Less than $2000
    (2) 2000-2499
    (3) 2500-2999
    (4) 3000-3499
    (5) 3500-3999
    (6) 4000-4499
    (7) 4500-4999
    (8) 5000 or more

17. What is the approximate number of students in your school *district*?
    (1) Less than 1,000
    (2) 1,000-4,999
    (3) 5,000-9,999
    (4) 10,000-14,999
    (5) 15,000-19,999
    (6) 20,000-24,999
    (7) 25,000-29,999
    (8) 30,000-34,999
    (9) 35,000 or more

18. What grades are included in the middle level school of which you are principal?
    (1) 7-8-9
    (2) 6-7-8
    (3) 5-6-7
    (4) 5-6-7-8
    (5) 6-7-8-9
    (6) 5-6
    (7) 6-7
    (8) 7-8
    (9) 8-9
    (10) Other:_____

19. Which of the following population categories best describes the locality of the middle level school of which you are principal?
    (1) City, more than 1,000,000
    (2) City, 150,000 to 999,999
    (3) Suburban, related to city of 150,000 population or more
    (4) City, 25,000 to 149,999 population, distinct from a metropolitan area
    (5) City, 5,000 to 24,999, not suburban
    (6) Town or rural under 5,000

20. In which geographical region is your school located?
    (1) New England
    (2) Mid-Atlantic
    (3) South
    (4) Midwest
    (5) Southwest
    (6) Rocky Mountain
    (7) West Coast
    (8) Alaska or Hawaii

21. Is your school accredited by a regional accrediting association?
    (1) Yes
    (2) No

School Leadership Questions

22. During the school year, on the average, how many hours a week do you work at your job as principal?
    (1) Less than 40   (2) 40-49   (3) 50-59   (4) 60-69   (5) 70 or more

23. How do you spend your time during the typical work week? Rank these nine areas according to the amount of time spent in each area. In Column A, mark a "1" next to the area in which you *do spend* the most time, ranking all areas until you have marked a "9" next to the area in which you spend the least time. Then in Column B, mark a "1" next to the area in which you feel you *should spend* the most time, ranking all items until you have marked "9" next to the area in which you feel you should spend the least time.

A. *Do Spend Time*	*Area of Responsibility*	B. *Should Spend Time*
_____	(1) *Community* (PTA, advisory groups, parent conferences, etc.)	_____
_____	(2) *District Office* (meetings, task forces, reports, etc.)	_____
_____	(3) *Personnel* (evaluating, advising, conferring, recruiting, etc.)	_____
_____	(4) *Planning* (annual, long range)	_____
_____	(5) *Professional Development* (reading, conferences, etc.)	_____
_____	(6) *Program Development* (curriculum, instructional leadership, etc.)	_____

(Question continued on next page.)

A. Do Spend Time	Area of Responsibility	B. Should Spend Time
_____	(7) *School Management* (weekly calendar, office, budget, memos, etc.)	_____
_____	(8) *Student Activities* (meetings, supervision, planning, etc.)	_____
_____	(9) *Student Behavior* (discipline, attendance, meetings, etc.)	_____

24. To what extent do you *participate in determining* the budget allocation for your school?
    (1) High participation   (3) Little participation
    (2) Moderate partici-   (4) No participation
        pation

25. To what extent do you *have the authority to approve* the allocation of discretionary funds within your school budget; i.e., how much autonomy or latitude do you have in the allocation of monies which are available to your building?
    (1)   Unrestricted authority
    (2)   Authority with some restriction, such as approval by superiors
    (3)   No authority

26. Various individuals or groups are important to the decision-making process at the building level. Consider the types of decisions in the left-hand column and then indicate the degree of involvement of each person(s) in the appropriate box. *Mark a "1"* in the cell to indicate those who discuss the decision; *Mark a "2"* for those who make recommendations; *Mark a "3"* for those who make the actual decision; *Mark a "0"* if there is no involvement.

    Thus: 0 = *No involvement*   2 = *Make recommendations*
            1 = *Involved in discussion*   3 = *Make decision*

	Principal	Assistant Principal	Leadership Team	Team Ldrs. Dept. Chairs	Staff Committees	Faculty as a Whole	Individual Teacher	Students	Parents/ Community	Central Office	School Board
(1) Adding a new course or instructional program											
(2) Adopting rules for student behavior											
(3) Curricular reform											
(4) Developing a budget for your school											
(5) Evaluating teaching staff											
(6) Evaluating the school's grading practices											
(7) Formulating school goals & mission											
(8) Hiring teaching staff											
(9) School organization (teams vs. depts.)											

Duties and responsibilities of Assistant Principals.

27. Principals have final responsibility for everything that happens in a school, but assistant principals share in differing degrees in that responsibility. Please indicate the job profile of the assistant principal in your school to whom you gave the Assistant Principal Form of this survey (blue survey form). If you do not have an assistant principal, mark the following box and go to the next question.
    ☐ No Assistant Principal in this school.

Responsibility. Please circle the number which indicates the degree of responsibility the assistant principal has for each job function. Use the following scale:

(1) Minor Responsibility—Principal does the job; AP may provide assistance at principal's discretion.
(2) Moderate Responsibility—The job is delegated but is closely supervised; principal and AP work together.
(3) Major Responsibility—The job is delegated and not closely supervised; AP is held responsible for the job.

Importance. Please circle the number which indicates the degree of importance the delegated duty has to the effective functioning of the school. Use the following scale:

(1) Minor importance—The job is not very important. If it is not completed effectively, there will not be a significant negative effect on overall school effectiveness.
(2) Moderate importance—The job is important. If it is not completed effectively, the overall effectiveness of the school is diminished.
(3) Major importance—The job is critical. If it is not completed effectively, the overall effectiveness of the school is significantly impaired.

Degree of Discretionary Behavior. Please circle the number which indicates the degree of discretionary behavior associated with the job function. Use the following scale:

(1) Minor discretionary behavior—The behavior needed to complete the function is almost completely dictated by others; the AP makes few, if any decisions.
(2) Moderate discretionary behavior—The behavior needed to complete the function is generally self-directing, with little direction from others. The AP has the opportunity to make most decisions associated with this function.
(3) Major discretionary behavior—The behavior needed to complete the function is completely self-directing. The AP receives no direction from others and make all decisions associated with this function.

Not Applicable. Please circle the "0" for any job function that does not apply in your school.

DUTIES:	Not Applicable	Responsibility			Importance			Discretionary Behavior		
		Minor	Moderate	Major	Minor	Moderate	Major	Minor	Moderate	Major
(1) Adviser/Advisee Program	0	1	2	3	1	2	3	1	2	3
(2) Articulation with Elementary School	0	1	2	3	1	2	3	1	2	3
(3) Articulation with High School	0	1	2	3	1	2	3	1	2	3
(4) Building Use/Calendar	0	1	2	3	1	2	3	1	2	3
(5) Community Relations	0	1	2	3	1	2	3	1	2	3
(6) Cocurricular Activities	0	1	2	3	1	2	3	1	2	3
(7) Curriculum	0	1	2	3	1	2	3	1	2	3
(8) Department Teams	0	1	2	3	1	2	3	1	2	3
(9) Discipline/Attendance	0	1	2	3	1	2	3	1	2	3
(10) Guidance/Health Service	0	1	2	3	1	2	3	1	2	3
(11) Instructional Improvement	0	1	2	3	1	2	3	1	2	3
(12) Instructional Materials	0	1	2	3	1	2	3	1	2	3
(13) Interdisciplinary Teams	0	1	2	3	1	2	3	1	2	3
(14) Interscholastic Athletics	0	1	2	3	1	2	3	1	2	3
(15) Parental Involvement/Volunteers	0	1	2	3	1	2	3	1	2	3
(16) Scheduling	0	1	2	3	1	2	3	1	2	3
(17) School Goal Setting	0	1	2	3	1	2	3	1	2	3
(18) Staff Development	0	1	2	3	1	2	3	1	2	3
(19) Support/Non-instructional Staff	0	1	2	3	1	2	3	1	2	3
(20) Transportation	0	1	2	3	1	2	3	1	2	3

28. Rate the following as they contributed to your preparation as principal.

	None	Little or Moderate	Great	Never Held
(1) Work as an assistant principal	1	2	3	0
(2) Work as a teacher	1	2	3	0
(3) Work as an adviser of a student activity	1	2	3	0
(4) Work as a guidance counselor	1	2	3	0
(5) Work as a department head or team leader	1	2	3	0
(6) Work as a member of a school leadership team	1	2	3	0
(7) Participation in community activities	1	2	3	0
(8) Participation in professional activities	1	2	3	0
(9) University coursework	1	2	3	0
(10) University field experiences	1	2	3	0

29. What is your perception of the importance of the following items as they contributed to your first appointment to the principalship?

	Little or No Importance	Somewhat Important	Very Important
(1) Amount and quality of professional preparation	1	2	3
(2) Assessment Center report	1	2	3
(3) Contacts outside the profession	1	2	3
(4) Contacts within the profession	1	2	3
(5) I was at the right spot at the right time	1	2	3
(6) Number of years of teaching experience	1	2	3
(7) Number of years of experience as an assistant principal	1	2	3
(8) Performance in formal assignments outside the classroom	1	2	3
(9) Performance in informal assignments outside the classroom	1	2	3
(10) Performance on competitive exams	1	2	3
(11) Success as a teacher	1	2	3
(12) Success as a counselor, librarian, etc.	1	2	3
(13) Success as an assistant principal	1	2	3
(14) Successful job interview	1	2	3
(15) The superintendent or assistant superintendent wanted me	1	2	3
(16) Other: _____	1	2	3

30. To what extent did the following individuals affect the final decision by which you were appointed principal?

	Little or No Influence	Moderate Influence	Great Influence
(1) Assistant Superintendent	1	2	3
(2) Superintendent of the district	1	2	3
(3) Board of Education	1	2	3
(4) University Professor	1	2	3
(5) Other professional contacts	1	2	3
(6) Friends	1	2	3
(7) Other: _____	1	2	3

31. To what degree have the circumstances listed below affected your decisions to change or not change school districts?

	Little or No Influence	Moderate Influence	Great Influence
(1) Family commitment (i.e. children, relatives) motivated me to pass up or not seek opportunities in other districts.	1	2	3
(2) Desire to live in a certain part of the country made me more place-oriented than career-oriented.	1	2	3
(3) The school environment (e.g., student discipline, parental views) has always been an important factor in my selection of jobs.	1	2	3
(4) Commitment to the middle level of education has caused me to remain at this level rather than change positions.	1	2	3

(5) Job security, seniority, and retirement benefits outweigh the advantages that might ensue from changing school districts.   1   2   3

(6) Other:_____   1   2   3

32. Please rate your degree of job satisfaction with your job environment as principal.

Satisfaction with:	Dissatisfied	Satisfied	Very Satisfied	Unsure
(1) The realization of expectations you had when you took the job	1	2	3	0
(2) The amount of time you devote to the job	1	2	3	0
(3) The results that you achieve	1	2	3	0
(4) The salary you receive	1	2	3	0
(5) The working conditions	1	2	3	0
(6) The amount of assistance you receive from your immediate supervisor	1	2	3	0
(7) The rapport you have with your supervisor	1	2	3	0
(8) The rapport you have with your administrative colleagues	1	2	3	0
(9) The rapport you have with teachers	1	2	3	0
(10) The rapport you have with students	1	2	3	0
(11) The rapport you have with parents and members of the community	1	2	3	0

Educational Program Questions

33. While a variety of terms may be used to describe a school's academic schedule (e.g., block, flexible, modular), most schools have a specific number of periods per day. How many instructional periods does your school schedule have? *Select only one answer.*

(1) Five   (2) Six   (3) Seven   (4) Eight   (5) Other:_____

34. What is the length of your school's basic instructional period?

(1) 40 minutes   (4) 51-55 minutes
(2) 41-45 minutes   (5) 56-60 minutes
(3) 46-50 minutes   (6) 61 minutes or more

35. In your school, what is the classroom teacher to pupil ratio for the current school year? *Select the one alternative that comes closest to your ratio.*

(1) 1 teacher for 10 or fewer students   (5) 1 teacher for 26 to 30 students
(2) 1 teacher for 11 to 15 students   (6) 1 teacher for 31 to 35 students
(3) 1 teacher for 16 to 20 students   (7) 1 teacher for 36 to 40 students
(4) 1 teacher for 21 to 25 students   (8) 1 teacher for 41 or more students

36. Listed below are content areas often included in middle level curriculum. Circle the choice which corresponds to the grade(s) at which these content areas are taught in your school. Indicate by grade level if the content area is taught as a "required," or an "elective," or both. The example is for a school with grades 6-7-8. Home Economics is *required* in grade 6, *required and elective* in grade 7, and an *elective* in grade 8.

CONTENT AREA	Grade-5 Req.	Req.	Grade-6 Req.	Req.	Grade-7 Req.	Elec.	Grade-8 Req.	Elec.	Grade-9 Req.	Elec.
EXAMPLE: Home Economics	(1)	(2)	((3))	(4)	((5))	((6))	(7)	((8))	(9)	(0)
(1) English/Language Arts	(1)	(2)	(3)	(4)	(5)	(6)	(7)	(8)	(9)	(0)
(2) Mathematics	(1)	(2)	(3)	(4)	(5)	(6)	(7)	(8)	(9)	(0)
(3) Science	(1)	(2)	(3)	(4)	(5)	(6)	(7)	(8)	(9)	(0)
(4) Social Studies	(1)	(2)	(3)	(4)	(5)	(6)	(7)	(8)	(9)	(0)
(5) Reading	(1)	(2)	(3)	(4)	(5)	(6)	(7)	(8)	(9)	(0)
(6) Physical Education	(1)	(2)	(3)	(4)	(5)	(6)	(7)	(8)	(9)	(0)
(7) Health Education	(1)	(2)	(3)	(4)	(5)	(6)	(7)	(8)	(9)	(0)
(8) Sex Education	(1)	(2)	(3)	(4)	(5)	(6)	(7)	(8)	(9)	(0)
(9) Spelling	(1)	(2)	(3)	(4)	(5)	(6)	(7)	(8)	(9)	(0)
(10) Typing/Key-Boarding	(1)	(2)	(3)	(4)	(5)	(6)	(7)	(8)	(9)	(0)

		(1)	(2)	(3)	(4)	(5)	(6)	(7)	(8)	(9)	(0)
(11)	Computer Education	(1)	(2)	(3)	(4)	(5)	(6)	(7)	(8)	(9)	(0)
(12)	Art	(1)	(2)	(3)	(4)	(5)	(6)	(7)	(8)	(9)	(0)
(13)	Crafts	(1)	(2)	(3)	(4)	(5)	(6)	(7)	(8)	(9)	(0)
(14)	Foreign Language	(1)	(2)	(3)	(4)	(5)	(6)	(7)	(8)	(9)	(0)
(15)	Family Living Home Econ.	(1)	(2)	(3)	(4)	(5)	(6)	(7)	(8)	(9)	(0)
(16)	Industrial Education	(1)	(2)	(3)	(4)	(5)	(6)	(7)	(8)	(9)	(0)
(17)	Vocal Music	(1)	(2)	(3)	(4)	(5)	(6)	(7)	(8)	(9)	(0)
(18)	Chorus	(1)	(2)	(3)	(4)	(5)	(6)	(7)	(8)	(9)	(0)
(19)	Instrumental Music	(1)	(2)	(3)	(4)	(5)	(6)	(7)	(8)	(9)	(0)
(20)	Orchestra	(1)	(2)	(3)	(4)	(5)	(6)	(7)	(8)	(9)	(0)
(21)	General Music	(1)	(2)	(3)	(4)	(5)	(6)	(7)	(8)	(9)	(0)
(22)	Speech	(1)	(2)	(3)	(4)	(5)	(6)	(7)	(8)	(9)	(0)
(23)	Drama	(1)	(2)	(3)	(4)	(5)	(6)	(7)	(8)	(9)	(0)
(24)	Career Education	(1)	(2)	(3)	(4)	(5)	(6)	(7)	(8)	(9)	(0)
(25)	Study Skills	(1)	(2)	(3)	(4)	(5)	(6)	(7)	(8)	(9)	(0)
(26)	Agriculture	(1)	(2)	(3)	(4)	(5)	(6)	(7)	(8)	(9)	(0)
(27)	Journalism	(1)	(2)	(3)	(4)	(5)	(6)	(7)	(8)	(9)	(0)
(28)	Creative Education	(1)	(2)	(3)	(4)	(5)	(6)	(7)	(8)	(9)	(0)
(29)	Photography	(1)	(2)	(3)	(4)	(5)	(6)	(7)	(8)	(9)	(0)
(30)	Other:_____	(1)	(2)	(3)	(4)	(5)	(6)	(7)	(8)	(9)	(0)

37. Using the key listed below, please circle the numbers which best describe the grade reporting procedures used in your school to report pupil progress to parents for the basic subject areas of Language Arts, Math, Science, and Social Studies. *Circle all numbers that apply for each grade level.*

(1) Letter Scale
(2) Word Scale (e.g., Excellent, Good)
(3) Number Scale (e.g., 1-5)
(4) Satisfactory-Unsatisfactory; Pass-Fail

(5) Informal written notes
(6) Percentage marks (e.g., 86%)
(7) Progress in relation to potential
(8) Other:_____

Grade Reporting System

(1) Grade 5	1	2	3	4	5	6	7	8		(4) Grade 8	1	2	3	4	5	6	7	8
(2) Grade 6	1	2	3	4	5	6	7	8		(5) Grade 9	1	2	3	4	5	6	7	8
(3) Grade 7	1	2	3	4	5	6	7	8										

38. Four organizational formats are commonly employed for instruction in middle level education. For the five subject areas listed below, please identify the type of organizational format used to teach the *majority of students at each grade level* in your school. Mark *only* the grades in your school. The four organizational formats are:

(1) **Self-contained classroom** (one teacher teaches more than one subject to the same group of students)
(2) **Interdisciplinary teaming** (two or more teachers work together as a team to teach more than one subject to the same group of students)
(3) Period by period **departmentalized instruction** (a teacher teaches a subject to a different group of students period by period and that teacher is not part of a team for that subject)
(4) **Disciplinary Teaming** (two or more teachers work together as a team to teach the same subject to a group of students)

Circle the "0" if the subject is not taught at that grade.

The example below is for a school with grades 5-6-7-8. Mathematics is taught to most students using a self-contained classroom format in grade 5, an interdisciplinary teaming format in grade 6, a departmentalized period by period and subject by subject format in grade 7, and a disciplinary teaming format in grade 8.

SUBJECT AREA:	GRADE-5	GRADE-6	GRADE-7	GRADE-8	GRADE-9
EXAMPLE: Mathematics	0 ① 2 3 4	0 1 ② 3 4	0 1 2 ③ 4	0 1 2 3 ④	0 1 2 3 4
(1) English/Language Arts	0 1 2 3 4	0 1 2 3 4	0 1 2 3 4	0 1 2 3 4	0 1 2 3 4
(2) Mathematics	0 1 2 3 4	0 1 2 3 4	0 1 2 3 4	0 1 2 3 4	0 1 2 3 4
(3) Science	0 1 2 3 4	0 1 2 3 4	0 1 2 3 4	0 1 2 3 4	0 1 2 3 4
(4) Social Science	0 1 2 3 4	0 1 2 3 4	0 1 2 3 4	0 1 2 3 4	0 1 2 3 4
(5) Reading	0 1 2 3 4	0 1 2 3 4	0 1 2 3 4	0 1 2 3 4	0 1 2 3 4

39. Listed below are cocurricular activities often associated with middle level education. Identify the grade level at which students in your school are permitted to participate in these activities.

ACTIVITY	GRADE 5	GRADE 6	GRADE 7	GRADE 8	GRADE 9
(1) Career Days	1	2	3	4	5
(2) Debate	1	2	3	4	5
(3) Drama	1	2	3	4	5
(4) Honor Societies	1	2	3	4	5
(5) Intramural Sports	1	2	3	4	5
(6) Minicourses	1	2	3	4	5
(7) Musical Groups	1	2	3	4	5
(8) Publications	1	2	3	4	5
(9) Student Clubs	1	2	3	4	5
(10) Student Government	1	2	3	4	5
(11) Other:_____	1	2	3	4	5

Issues and Trends Questions

40. What do you think is the ideal grade organizational structure for a middle level school?
   (1) 7-8-9
   (2) 6-7-8
   (3) 5-6-7
   (4) 5-6-7-8
   (5) 6-7-8-9
   (6) 5-6
   (7) 6-7
   (8) 7-8
   (9) 8-9
   (10) Other:_____
   (3) Grades 7 and below
   (4) Grades 6 and below
   (5) Grade 5

43. In your opinion, what is occurring with regard to parent, citizen, and student involvement in your school? Use this present school year as the basis for your response.
   A. The desire of parents to participate is
      (1) increasing over previous years
      (2) decreasing from previous years
      (3) about the same as in previous years.
   B. The desire of citizens other than parents to participate is
      (1) increasing over previous years
      (2) decreasing from previous years
      (3) about the same as in previous years.

41. All things considered (learning conditions, teaching staff, capital outlay, etc.), what is your judgment about the optimum number of students for a middle level school?
   (1) Less than 200
   (2) 200-399
   (3) 400-599
   (4) 600-799
   (5) 800-999
   (6) 1000-1199
   (7) 1200-1399
   (8) 1400-1599
   (9) 1600-1799
   (10) 1800-1999
   (11) 2000 or more

42. Identify any grade levels at which you feel greater emphasis should be placed upon intramural rather than interscholastic activities.
   (1) All middle level grades
   (2) Grades 8 and below

44. Listed below are community groups which may have sought, successfully or unsuccessfully, to bring about changes in the operation of your school. Mark the choice which best indicates the extent of influence of each interest group on your school during the past two years.

INTEREST GROUP	Little/No Influence	Moderate Influence	Extreme Influence
(1) Censorship groups (books, programs, etc.)	1	2	3
(2) Citizen or parent groups (non PTA)	1	2	3
(3) Extreme left-wing individuals/groups	1	2	3
(4) Extreme right-wing individuals/groups	1	2	3
(5) Individuals/groups concerned about national reports, studies	1	2	3
(6) Legal aid groups	1	2	3
(7) Local elementary schools	1	2	3
(8) Local high schools	1	2	3
(9) Local media (editorial policy)	1	2	3
(10) PTA or PTO	1	2	3
(11) Religious or church organizations	1	2	3
(12) State colleges and/or universities	1	2	3
(13) Teachers' association or union	1	2	3
(14) The business community	1	2	3
(15) Women's rights or minority organizations	1	2	3
(16) Other:_____	1	2	3

45. Does your school have some system of individualized promotion for students rather than the customary grade placement and year-end promotion?
    (1) Yes (please describe briefly) _____
    (2) No, we do not have individualized promotion
    (3) No, we do not have individualized promotion, but I would like us to move in that direction.

46. In recent years technological advancements (e.g., satellite communication, instructional television, computer-assisted instruction) have provided schools with opportunities for instructional methods not used 10 or 20 years ago. Do you believe educational technology *has improved* the quality of learning experiences for students of your school?
    (1) Yes   (2) No

47. Do you believe educational technology *will improve* the quality of educational instruction for future students of your school?
    (1) Yes   (2) No

48. Please indicate the degree to which *you believe* the middle level characteristics listed below are important to an instructionally effective middle level school. Then, indicate the degree to which *your school currently implements* those middle level characteristics. Finally, please identify the *plans you have* in your school to implement each characteristic.

CATEGORY DESCRIPTIONS:
Importance of Characteristic. Use the following scale to describe the degree of importance of each characteristic in an instructionally effective middle level school.

(1) Little or no importance—absence of this characteristic will not affect the operation of the school.
(2) Somewhat important—presence of this characteristic adds to the quality of the school.
(3) Very important—presence of this characteristic is critical to a quality school.

Current Implementation: Use the following scale to describe the degree of implementation of each characteristic.
(1) No implementation—we do not have this characteristic in our school.
(2) Partial implementation—we implement this characteristic but not every aspect as it is described in the statement.
(3) Full implementation—we implement every aspect of the characteristic as described in the statement.

Plans for Implementation. Use the following scale to describe the plans you have in your school for implementing the characteristic.
(1) We implement the characteristic fully and plan to continue to do so.
(2) We implement the characteristic fully but plan to discontinue doing so in the next two years.
(3) We do not implement the characteristic fully but already have plans to do so in the next two years.
(4) We do not implement the characteristic fully but are considering full implementation in the next two years.
(5) We do not implement the characteristic fully and plan to continue as we are for the next two years.

CHARACTERISTIC:	Importance of Characteristic	Current Implementation	Plans for Implementation
(1) Interdisciplinary teams of 2-5 teachers sharing common students, common planning time, and housed in close proximity.	1 2 3	1 2 3	1 2 3 4 5
(2) Exploratory course offerings which provide required (not elective) curricular opportunities for all students (e.g., computers, family living, industrial technology, music).	1 2 3	1 2 3	1 2 3 4 5
(3) Adviser-advisee program regularly scheduled for 15 minutes or more during each classroom day.	1 2 3	1 2 3	1 2 3 4 5
(4) Cocurricular program separate from regular graded courses, but occurring during the school day, designed to provide students with the opportunity to pursue leadership roles, special interests, and socialization.	1 2 3	1 2 3	1 2 3 4 5
(5) Intramural activities offered for all students during or immediately after the regular classroom day.	1 2 3	1 2 3	1 2 3 4 5

49. Listed below are several factors which could be considered "roadblocks" preventing principals from doing the job they would like to do. Indicate the degree to which each factor has or has not been a roadblock to you as principal over the past two years.

FACTOR	Not a Factor	Moderate Factor	Serious Factor
(1) Collective bargaining agreement	1	2	3
(2) Deficient communication among administrative levels	1	2	3
(3) Inability to obtain funding	1	2	3
(4) Inability to provide teacher time for planning or professional development	1	2	3
(5) Insufficient space and physical facilities	1	2	3
(6) Lack of competent administrative assistance	1	2	3
(7) Lack of competent office help	1	2	3
(8) Lack of data about student skills and styles	1	2	3
(9) Lack of data on program successes/failures	1	2	3
(10) Lack of district-wide flexibility (all schools conform to same policy)	1	2	3
(11) Lack of knowledge among staff regarding program for middle level students	1	2	3
(12) Lack of time for myself	1	2	3
(13) Long-standing tradition in the school/district	1	2	3
(14) Parents apathetic or irresponsible about their children	1	2	3
(15) Pressure from community	1	2	3
(16) Problem students (apathetic, hostile, etc.)	1	2	3
(17) Regulations or mandates from state or district governing boards	1	2	3
(18) Resistance to change by staff	1	2	3
(19) Superintendent or central office staff	1	2	3
(20) Teacher tenure	1	2	3
(21) Teacher turnover	1	2	3
(22) Time required to administer/supervise extracurricular activities	1	2	3
(23) Time taken by administrative detail at expense of more important matters	1	2	3
(24) Too large a student body	1	2	3
(25) Too small a student body	1	2	3
(26) Variations in the ability and dedication of staff	1	2	3

50. Choose one:
   (1) The principal should establish the agenda and decide the important issues in the school.
   (2) The principal should share the decision making with the faculty on important school issues.

51. Choose one:
   (1) The principal should effectively and efficiently manage the day-by-day operation of the school.
   (2) The principal should provide leadership for the school based upon his/her best professional judgment.

52. Choose one:
   (1) The principal primarily should represent the interests of parents, leaders, and patrons of the school.
   (2) The principal should take the initiative in developing and implementing school policy according to his/her best professional judgment.

53. In recent years, the issue of teacher preparation has been a topic of much interest. Which of the following best describe the method(s) by which your teachers have been prepared to teach, specifically, at the middle level? *Circle more than one if appropriate.*
   (1) Inservice programs
   (2) Student/practice teaching at middle level
   (3) Courses at the university which focus on middle level education
   (4) Personal study
   (5) Other:_____
   (6) Generally, the staff has not had special preparation to teach at the middle level

54. Please identify the *three* most important skills/characteristics of an "excellent" middle level teacher. *Circle only three.*
    (1) Competence in subject matter knowledge
    (2) Competence in use of varied and developmentally appropriate methods of instruction
    (3) Competence in adjusting instruction to the varying learning styles and learning skills of the students
    (4) Competence in developing a positive relationship with students in the classroom.
    (5) Competence in counseling students
    (6) Competence in working as a team member
    (7) Competence in using positive methods for student discipline
    (8) Competence in promoting positive student self-concept
    (9) Competence in employee behaviors and work habits (dependability, punctuality, attendance)
    (10) Competence in working with parents
    (11) Competence in working with colleagues

55. Which of the following best describes your district's legal status on collective bargaining? *Select only one answer.*
    (1) No collective bargaining
    (2) Collective bargaining with teachers only
    (3) Collective bargaining with administrators only
    (4) Collective bargaining with teachers and administrators
    (5) Collective bargaining with all employees

56. Which of the following best describe the impact of collective bargaining in your school? *Circle all that apply.*
    (1) No collective bargaining
    (2) Enhanced my relationships with teachers
    (3) No appreciable effect on my relationship with teachers
    (4) Caused my relationships with teachers to deteriorate
    (5) Enhanced our ability to provide educational programs designed specifically for middle level students
    (6) No appreciable effect on our ability to provide educational programs designed specifically for middle level students
    (7) Lessened our ability to provide educational programs designed for middle level students.

57. Much has been written about the tasks of American schools. Please rank the 11 statements below according to *your belief* about their relative importance as educational purposes.

Assign a rank of "1" to the statement you consider most important, a rank of "2" to the next most important, until you assign a rank of "11" to the statement you consider least important.

____ (1) Acquisition of basic skills (reading, writing, speaking, computing, etc.)
____ (2) Appreciation for and experience with the fine arts
____ (3) Career planning and training in beginning occupational skills
____ (4) Development of moral and spiritual values
____ (5) Development of positive self-concept and good human relations
____ (6) Development of skills and practice in critical intellectual inquiry and problem solving
____ (7) Development of the skills to function in a technological society (engineering, scientific, etc.)
____ (8) Knowledge about and skills in preparation for family life (sex education, home management, problems of aging, etc.)
____ (9) Preparation for a changing world
____ (10) Physical fitness and useful leisure time sports
____ (11) Understanding of the American value system (its political, economic, social values, etc.)

**Thank you for taking the time to complete this survey!
Please return the survey in the envelope provided.**

National Association of Secondary School Principals

A National Study of Leadership In Middle Level Education

Principal Survey: Form B

Directions

Your questionnaire is identified by the label placed on it. It is not necessary to sign or place your name on the questionnaire. In reporting results, only statistical summaries of the responses of groups of principals will be cited. In no case will the identity of an individual be divulged. You are urged to make every answer a sincere one.

Circle the number of the appropriate response using pen or pencil. If you change a response, please make the change obvious so there is no doubt about how you wish to answer.

Please attempt to answer every question. For some questions none of the alternatives may correspond exactly to your situation, or to the opinion you hold. In such cases mark the alternative which comes closest to the answer you would like to give.

For the purposes of this study, two terms should be clarified:
  (1) **Middle level education** is a general phase used to encompass various combinations of grades five through nine.
  (2) **Principal** refers to the chief building administrator and should not be confused with the assistant principal or vice principal.

The cover letter provided criteria for determining whether the Assistant Principal (blue form) and the Leadership Team (green form) should be distributed in your school. Please indicate below whether you did or did not distribute the two surveys and the job title of the person(s) to whom you gave them.

☐ I gave the Assistant Principal Survey to: (job title)_____.
☐ I did not distribute the Assistant Principal Survey.
☐ I gave the Leadership Team Survey to: (job title)_____.
☐ I did not distribute the Leadership Team Survey.

Return your completed questionnaire to NASSP in the envelope provided. Thank you for your participation in this important study.

Please Return This Questionnaire Within 10 Days

Advisory Committee for the National Study of Leadership in Middle Level Education:
James Anding, Nathan Hale Junior High School, Omaha, NE; James Aseltine, Irving Robbins Middle School, Farmington, CT; Don Dalton, Canyon Vista Middle School, Austin, TX; Marion Payne, Owen Brown Middle School, Columbia, MD; Lori Simmons, Commodore Bainbridge Middle School, Bainbridge Island, WA; Joseph Tafoya, Santa Ana Unified School District, Santa Ana, CA; Sue Carol Thompson, Blue Valley School District, Overland Park, KS.

Research Team:

Donald Clark, University of Arizona; Judith Irvin, Florida State University; James Keefe, NASSP; George Melton, NASSP Emeritus; Jerry Valentine, University of Missouri

Demographic and Control Questions

1. What is your sex?
   - (1) Male
   - (2) Female

2. What is your age?
   - (1) 24 and under
   - (2) 25-29
   - (3) 30-34
   - (4) 35-39
   - (5) 40-44
   - (6) 45-49
   - (7) 50-54
   - (8) 55-59
   - (9) 60 or older

3. With what ethnic group would you identify your-self?
   - (1) White
   - (2) Black
   - (3) Chicano/Hispanic
   - (4) American Indian
   - (5) Asian
   - (6) Other:_____

4. How many years have you been a principal of this school, including this current year?
   - (1) One
   - (2) Two
   - (3) Three
   - (4) 4-5
   - (5) 6-8
   - (6) 9-11
   - (7) 12-14
   - (8) 15-17
   - (9) 18 or more

5. How many total years have you served as a principal of this and other schools, including this current year?
   - (1) One
   - (2) 2-3
   - (3) 4-5
   - (4) 6-7
   - (5) 8-9
   - (6) 10-14
   - (7) 15-19
   - (8) 20-24
   - (9) 25 or more

6. In which of the following areas did you major as an undergraduate? *Select only one answer.*
   - (1) Mathematics
   - (2) Physical or biological sciences
   - (3) Social sciences (sociology, history, etc.)
   - (4) Humanities (literature, languages, etc.)
   - (5) Physical education
   - (6) Business
   - (7) Fine arts
   - (8) Vocational-Technical (home economics, industrial arts, etc.)
   - (9) Elementary education
   - (10) Secondary education (other than physical education)
   - (11) Middle level education
   - (12) Other:_____

7. What is your major field of *graduate* study? *Choose only one answer.*
   - (1) Educational administration and supervision
   - (2) Secondary education, curriculum and instruction
   - (3) Middle level education, curriculum and instruction
   - (4) Elementary education, curriculum and instruction
   - (5) Guidance and counseling
   - (6) Physical education
   - (7) Some other educational specialty:_____
   - (8) Humanities, social sciences, or fine arts
   - (9) Math or sciences
   - (10) Business
   - (11) Other:_____
   - (12) No graduate study

8. What is your career plan for the next 3-5 years? *Select one.*
   - (1) Remain in present position
   - (2) Retirement
   - (3) Seek a position as superintendent
   - (4) Seek a central office position other than superintendent
   - (5) Seek a different position as a middle level principal
   - (6) Seek a position as an elementary principal
   - (7) Seek a position as a high school principal
   - (8) Seek a position in a junior college or university
   - (9) Seek a position in a state department of education or other educational service agency (other than a school district)
   - (10) Return to full time teaching
   - (11) Seek a position in a career field other than education
   - (12) I am undecided

9. In which of the following positions have you had one full year or more of experience? *Circle all that apply.*
   - (1) Athletic coach
   - (2) Athletic director
   - (3) Counselor or guidance position
   - (4) Dean or registrar
   - (5) Department chairperson
   - (6) Team leader

10. In addition to salary, which of the following fringe benefits do you receive from your school or district? *Circle all appropriate responses.*
    (1) No fringe benefits
    (2) Automobile/mileage allowance
    (3) Retirement
    (4) Dental insurance
    (5) Expense account
    (6) Housing or equivalent subsidy
    (7) Life insurance
    (8) Meals
    (9) Medical insurance
    (10) College tuition for yourself
    (11) Tuition for dependents (non-public)

11. Regardless of payment schedule, on what time period is your yearly salary contract based?
    (1) 12 months
    (2) 11½
    (3) 11
    (4) 10½
    (5) 10
    (6) 9½
    (7) 9

12. Is your contract multi-year?
    (1) No
    (2) Yes—two year contract
    (3) Yes—three year
    (4) Yes—more than three year

13. Which of the following categories best describes the middle level school of which you are principal? *Select only one.*
    (1) Public
    (2) Parochial or diocesan
    (3) Private, religious affiliated
    (4) Private, not religious affiliated
    (5) Other:_____

14. How many students are currently enrolled in your school?
    (1) Less than 200
    (2) 200-399
    (3) 400-599
    (4) 600-799
    (5) 800- 999
    (6) 1000-1199
    (7) 1200-1399
    (8) 1400-1599
    (9) 1600-1799
    (10) 1800-1999
    (11) 2000 or more

15. What was the average per pupil expenditure (exclusive of capital outlay) for each student in your school during the 1990-91 school year?
    (1) Less than $2000
    (2) 2000-2499
    (3) 2500-2999
    (4) 3000-3499
    (5) 3500-3999
    (6) 4000-4499
    (7) 4500-4999
    (8) 5000 or more

16. What is the approximate number of students in your school *district*?
    (1) Less than 1,000
    (2) 1,000-4,999
    (3) 5,000-9,999
    (4) 10,000-14,999
    (5) 15,000-19,999
    (6) 20,000-24,999
    (7) 25,000-29,999
    (8) 30,000-34,999
    (9) 35,000 plus

17. What grades are included in the middle level school of which you are principal?
    (1) 7-8-9
    (2) 6-7-8
    (3) 5-6-7
    (4) 5-6-7-8
    (5) 6-7-8-9
    (6) 5-6
    (7) 6-7
    (8) 7-8
    (9) 8-9
    (10) Other:_____

18. For how many years has your school operated under the current grade configuration; i.e., 7-8-9, or 5-6-7-8, or 7-8, etc.?
    (1) Less than 1 year
    (2) 1-5
    (3) 6-10
    (4) 11-15
    (5) 16-20
    (6) 21-25
    (7) 26-30
    (8) 31-50
    (9) More than 50

19. Which of the following population categories best describes the locality of the middle level school of which you are principal?
    (1) City, more than 1,000,000
    (2) City, 150,000 to 999,999
    (3) Suburban, related to city of 150,000 population or more
    (4) City, 25,000 to 149,999 population, distinct from a metropolitan area
    (5) City, 5,000 to 24,999, not suburban
    (6) Town or rural under 4,999

20. In which geographical region is your school located?
    (1) New England
    (2) Mid-Atlantic
    (3) South
    (4) Midwest
    (5) Southwest
    (6) Rocky Mountain
    (7) West Coast
    (8) Alaska or Hawaii

21. Is your school accredited by a regional accrediting association?
    (1) Yes
    (2) No

School Leadership Questions

22. Do you have a written job description for your position as principal?
    - (1) Yes
    - (2) No

23. How much authority do you have to *fill teacher vacancies? Select one.*
    - (1) I make the selection and the central office endorses it.
    - (2) I make the selection within limited options stipulated by the central office.
    - (3) I recommend a person to fill the vacancy and the central office makes the decision.
    - (4) The central office selects the teacher to fill the vacancy.

24. How much authority do you have to *make alternative personnel decisions* such as employing two or three teacher aides instead of one teacher?
    - (1) Unrestricted authority
    - (2) Authority with some restriction, such as approval by superiors
    - (3) No authority

The next two questions are about "leadership teams." Please respond according to the following definition of a "leadership team." A **leadership team** is a group of teachers and administrators designated by the principal or elected by the faculty to assist in the leadership operation of the school. These staff members may have been formally designated, or they may be a more informal group obviously instrumental in the on-going operation of the school. If you do not have a leadership team, mark the box below and go to question 27.

☐ We do not have a "leadership team" in our school.

25. How many people on your staff comprise your "leadership team"?
    - (1) One
    - (2) Two
    - (3) Three
    - (4) Four
    - (5) Five
    - (6) Six
    - (7) Seven
    - (8) More than seven

26. What are the job position titles of persons on your "leadership team"? *Circle all that apply.*
    - (1) teacher
    - (2) dean
    - (3) assistant principal
    - (4) administrative intern
    - (5) counselor
    - (6) coordinator
    - (7) director
    - (8) team leader
    - (9) Other:_____

27. Much is written about involving parents and other citizens in education. Please identify the area(s) in which you involve parents or other citizens in a *planning or advisory capacity* in your school. *Circle all appropriate responses.*
    - (1) Objectives and priorities for the school
    - (2) Program changes and new programs being considered
    - (3) Student activities
    - (4) Student behavior, rights, responsibilities
    - (5) Finance and fund raising
    - (6) Evaluation of programs
    - (7) Parents or other citizens are not involved in any of the above

28. Please circle all the areas in which you involve parents or other citizens in the *operation* of your school.
    - (1) Advisors, counselors to individual students
    - (2) Monitors, supervisors, ticket sellers, etc., for student activities
    - (3) Operators of concessions, etc., for the benefit of the school
    - (4) Resource persons to programs and activities, including instruction
    - (5) Sponsors/moderators of student groups
    - (6) Volunteer aides
    - (7) Volunteer tutors
    - (8) Other:_____

Duties and responsibilities of Assistant Principals.

29. Principals have final responsibility for everything that happens in a school, but assistant principals share in differing degrees in that responsibility. Please indicate the job profile of the assistant principal in your school to whom you gave the Assistant Principal Form of this survey (Blue Survey Form). If you do not have an assistant principal, mark the following box and go to the next question.

    ☐ No Assistant Principal in this school.

    Responsibility. Please circle the number which indicates the degree of responsibility the assistant principal has for each job function. Use the following scale:
    (1) Minor Responsibility—Principal does the job; AP may provide assistance at principal's discretion.
    (2) Moderate Responsibility—The job is delegated but is closely supervised; principal and AP work together.
    (3) Major Responsibility—The job is delegated and not closely supervised; AP is held responsible for the job.

Importance. Please circle the number which indicates the degree of importance the delegated duty has to the effective functioning of the school. Use the following scale:

(1) Minor importance—The job is not very important. If it is not completed effectively, there will not be a significant negative effect on overall school effectiveness.

(2) Moderate importance—The job is important. If it is not completed effectively, the overall effectiveness of the school is diminished.

(3) Major importance—The job is critical. If it is not completed effectively, the overall effectiveness of the school is significantly impaired.

Degree of Discretionary Behavior. Please circle the number which indicates the degree of discretionary behavior associated with the job function. Use the following scale:

(1) Minor discretionary behavior—The behavior needed to complete the function is almost completely dictated by others; the AP makes few, if any, decisions.

(2) Moderate discretionary behavior—The behavior needed to complete the function is generally self-directing, with little direction from others. The AP has the opportunity to make most decisions associated with this function.

(3) Major discretionary behavior—The behavior needed to complete the function is completely self-directing. The AP receives no direction from others and makes all decisions associated with this function.

Not Applicable. Please circle the "0" for any job function that does not apply.

AP DUTIES:	Not Applicable	Responsibility Minor	Responsibility Moderate	Responsibility Major	Importance Minor	Importance Moderate	Importance Major	Discretionary Behavior Minor	Discretionary Behavior Moderate	Discretionary Behavior Major
(1) Adviser/Advisee Program	0	1	2	3	1	2	3	1	2	3
(2) Articulation with Elementary School	0	1	2	3	1	2	3	1	2	3
(3) Articulation with High School	0	1	2	3	1	2	3	1	2	3
(4) Building Use/Calendar	0	1	2	3	1	2	3	1	2	3
(5) Cocurricular Activities	0	1	2	3	1	2	3	1	2	3
(6) Community Relations	0	1	2	3	1	2	3	1	2	3
(7) Curriculum	0	1	2	3	1	2	3	1	2	3
(8) Department Teams	0	1	2	3	1	2	3	1	2	3
(9) Discipline/Attendance	0	1	2	3	1	2	3	1	2	3
(10) Guidance/Health Service	0	1	2	3	1	2	3	1	2	3
(11) Instructional Improvement	0	1	2	3	1	2	3	1	2	3
(12) Instructional Materials	0	1	2	3	1	2	3	1	2	3
(13) Interdisciplinary Teams	0	1	2	3	1	2	3	1	2	3
(14) Interscholastic Athletics	0	1	2	3	1	2	3	1	2	3
(15) Parental Involvement/Volunteers	0	1	2	3	1	2	3	1	2	3
(16) Scheduling	0	1	2	3	1	2	3	1	2	3
(17) School Goal Setting	0	1	2	3	1	2	3	1	2	3
(18) Staff Development	0	1	2	3	1	2	3	1	2	3
(19) Support/Non-instructional Staff	0	1	2	3	1	2	3	1	2	3
(20) Transportation	0	1	2	3	1	2	3	1	2	3

30. What is the professional certification of the majority of your teachers?

    (1) Secondary   (3) Elementary

    (2) Middle level

31. What percent of your full-time teachers are women?

    (1) Less than 10%   (6) 50-59%

    (2) 10-19%   (7) 60-69%

    (3) 20-29%   (8) 70-79%

    (4) 30-39%   (9) 80-89%

    (5) 40-49%   (10) 90-100%

32. For the next question, circle the number which describes your perception of how your job actually is; then for the following question, circle the number which describes how you think your job should be.

How much prestige do you feel your position as principal *provides*?

1	2	3	4	5
Little		Moderate		Much

How much prestige do you feel your position as principal *should provide*?

1	2	3	4	5
Little		Moderate		Much

33. If you could choose again, would you select educational administration as a career?
    (1) Yes—definitely
    (2) Yes—probably
    (3) Uncertain
    (4) No—probably not
        (Why not:_____)
    (5) No—definitely not
        (Why not:_____)

34. Which of the following is most descriptive of the position held by the person who you believe most directly influenced your ability to function effectively during your initial year as a principal?
    (1) Another principal
    (2) A professor
    (3) A teacher(s)
    (4) A central office administrator
    (5) Other:_____
    (6) No one person was particularly influential

35. Rate the influence that the following groups or individuals had on your decision to enter educational administration.

	Little or No Influence	Moderate Influence	Great Influence	Unsure or Don't Know
(1) Parents	1	2	3	0
(2) Spouse	1	2	3	0
(3) Colleagues	1	2	3	0
(4) Professors	1	2	3	0
(5) An administrator	1	2	3	0
(6) Other_____	1	2	3	0

36. How *important* to you were the following statements about jobs and careers at the time that you decided to (a) enter teaching?   and (b) enter administration?

Teaching or Administration will:	A. TEACHING			B. ADMINISTRATION		
	Little/No Importance	Somewhat Important	Very Important	Little/No Importance	Somewhat Important	Very Important
(1) Provide an opportunity to make a good salary	1	2	3	1	2	3
(2) Provide an opportunity to use my special abilities and aptitudes	1	2	3	1	2	3
(3) Provide social status and prestige	1	2	3	1	2	3
(4) Provide opportunity to work with people rather than things	1	2	3	1	2	3
(5) Permit me to be creative and original	1	2	3	1	2	3
(6) Provide an opportunity to exercise leadership	1	2	3	1	2	3
(7) Provide a stable and secure future	1	2	3	1	2	3
(8) Provide the opportunity to be helpful to others	1	2	3	1	2	3
(9) Offer excellent hours and vacations	1	2	3	1	2	3
(10) Provide an opportunity to help students	1	2	3	1	2	3
(11) Offer recognition by others	1	2	3	1	2	3
(12) Provide opportunity to improve curriculum and instruction	1	2	3	1	2	3
(13) Other:_____	1	2	3	1	2	3

Educational Program Questions

37. If you have a gifted/talented program in your school, which of the following describes the organizational format of the program? *Circle all that apply.*
    (1) No gifted/talented program
    (2) Released time during school hours (special classes)
    (3) Regular class situation with individualized projects focusing specifically on the gifted/talented
    (4) After school, evening or weekend program
    (5) Summer program
    (6) Cooperative program with other school or organization
    (7) Other:_____

38. Ability grouping is the assignment of students to classes based upon academic ability. Which statement best describes ability grouping in your school (excluding special education classes)?
    (1) We have no form of grouping by academic ability
    (2) We group students into specific classes by academic ability; e.g., grouping for reading or math classes

    (3) We do not group students into specific classes by academic ability, but teachers do group their students by academic ability within specific classes.

39. Which of the following best describes the future of ability grouping in your school (exclusive of special education classes)? *Select only one answer.*
    (1) We have ability grouping and have no plans to change our current arrangements
    (2) We have ability grouping but are considering eliminating it
    (3) We have studied the issue and will eliminate ability grouping within the next year
    (4) We do not currently group by ability and plan to continue that way
    (5) We do not currently group by ability but are considering changing to ability grouping
    (6) We do not currently group by ability but we have studied the issue and will begin ability grouping within the next year.

40. Four organizational formats are commonly employed for instruction in middle level education. For the five subject areas listed below, please identify the type of organizational format used to teach the *majority of students at each grade level* in your school. Mark *only* the grades in your school. The four organizational formats are:

(1) **Self-contained classroom** (one teacher teaches more than one subject to the same group of students)

(2) **Interdisciplinary teaming** (two or more teachers work together as a team to teach more than one subject to the same group of students)

(3) Period by period **departmentalized instruction** (a teacher teaches a subject to a different group of students period by period and that teacher is not part of a team for that subject)

(4) **Disciplinary teaming** (two or more teachers work together as a team to teach the same subject to a group of students)

Circle the "0" if the subject is not taught at that grade.

The example below is for a school with grades 5-6-7-8. Mathematics is taught to most students using a self-contained classroom format in grade 5, an interdisciplinary teaming format in grade 6, a departmentalized period by period and subject by subject format in grade 7, and a disciplinary teaming format in grade 8.

SUBJECT AREA:	GRADE-5	GRADE-6	GRADE-7	GRADE-8	GRADE-9
EXAMPLE: Mathematics	0 ① 2 3 4	0 1 ② 3 4	0 1 2 ③ 4	0 1 2 3 ④	0 1 2 3 4
(1) English/Language Arts	0 1 2 3 4	0 1 2 3 4	0 1 2 3 4	0 1 2 3 4	0 1 2 3 4
(2) Mathematics	0 1 2 3 4	0 1 2 3 4	0 1 2 3 4	0 1 2 3 4	0 1 2 3 4
(3) Science	0 1 2 3 4	0 1 2 3 4	0 1 2 3 4	0 1 2 3 4	0 1 2 3 4
(4) Social Science	0 1 2 3 4	0 1 2 3 4	0 1 2 3 4	0 1 2 3 4	0 1 2 3 4
(5) Reading	0 1 2 3 4	0 1 2 3 4	0 1 2 3 4	0 1 2 3 4	0 1 2 3 4

If your school has one or more interdisciplinary teams of teachers working with an expanded group of students, please respond to the following 10 questions. If you do *not* have one or more interdisciplinary teams, mark this box ☐ and go to item 51.

41. We have interdisciplinary teams for grade(s):
    (1) 5
    (2) 6
    (3) 7
    (4) 8
    (5) 9

42. Our teams include the following subject areas:
    (1) Math, Science, Social Sciences, English/Language Arts
    (2) Math, Science, Social Sciences, English/Language Arts, Reading
    (3) Other:_____

43. Our team teachers have: (*Circle all that apply.*)
    (1) One planning period that is not necessarily at the same time for all members of the team
    (2) One planning period at the same time for all members of the team
    (3) One common planning period for all team members plus an individual planning period.

44. The students who are a part of a team:
    (1) Are taught only by the teachers of their team for a "teaming" subject
    (2) May be taught by a non-team teacher for a "teaming" subject (exclusive of special education)

45. Students are assigned to their respective team:
    (1) Heterogeneously (e.g., at random)
    (2) Homogeneously (e.g., by ability, by achievement, by interest)

46. Team leaders: (*Circle all that apply.*)
    (1) Are appointed by the administration
    (2) Are selected by the team members
    (3) Are rotated among the members of the team
    (4) Are given released time for team leader responsibilities (additional time compared to other team members)
    (5) Are given monetary compensation for their team leader responsibilities
    (6) We do not have a designated team leader.

47. Which of the following best describes the location of classrooms used by teachers who teach on the same team?
    (1) The classrooms of all teachers on the same team are adjacent
    (2) The classrooms of most teachers on the same team are adjacent
    (3) The classrooms of most teachers on the same team are not adjacent

48. When the teams of teachers were organized, what process was used to determine team membership?
    (1) The administration appointed the teams
    (2) The administration appointed the teams after input from the teachers
    (3) The teachers selected their own teams
    (4) Other:_____

49. How many interdisciplinary teams do you have in your school?
    (1) One
    (2) Two
    (3) Three
    (4) Four
    (5) Five
    (6) Six
    (7) Seven
    (8) Eight or more

50. What approximate percent of your students (excluding special education students) are receiving some of their instruction from an interdisciplinary teaching team?
    (1) 25% or Less
    (2) 26-50%
    (3) 51-75%
    (4) 76-100%

51. Listed below are sports often associated with middle level education. For the appropriate sports, circle the numbers which correspond to the grade level and the sex of the students permitted to participate in *interscholastic competition* (between schools) this year in your school.

SPORTS	GRADE 5 Boys	GRADE 5 Girls	GRADE 6 Boys	GRADE 6 Girls	GRADE 7 Boys	GRADE 7 Girls	GRADE 8 Boys	GRADE 8 Girls	GRADE 9 Boys	GRADE 9 Girls
(1) No interscholastic sports	1	2	3	4	5	6	7	8	9	0
(2) Baseball	1	2	3	4	5	6	7	8	9	0
(3) Basketball	1	2	3	4	5	6	7	8	9	0
(4) Football	1	2	3	4	5	6	7	8	9	0
(5) Gymnastics	1	2	3	4	5	6	7	8	9	0
(6) Ice Hockey	1	2	3	4	5	6	7	8	9	0
(7) Soccer	1	2	3	4	5	6	7	8	9	0
(8) Softball	1	2	3	4	5	6	7	8	9	0
(9) Swimming	1	2	3	4	5	6	7	8	9	0
(10) Tennis	1	2	3	4	5	6	7	8	9	0
(11) Track	1	2	3	4	5	6	7	8	9	0
(12) Volleyball	1	2	3	4	5	6	7	8	9	0
(13) Wrestling	1	2	3	4	5	6	7	8	9	0
(14) Other:_____	1	2	3	4	5	6	7	8	9	0

Issues and Trends Questions

52. If your school has adopted a "middle school" organizational plan which includes either grades 5-6-7-8 or 6-7-8, please circle all the reasons for adopting either of these two patterns. If your system has not changed to a middle school plan of grades 5-6-7-8 or 6-7-8, please circle item (10).
   (1) Provide a better transition from elementary to high school
   (2) Solve concerns about a junior high program
   (3) Employ new curriculum or instructional innovations
   (4) Utilize a new school facility or building
   (5) Adjust to enrollment trends
   (6) Employ ideas or programs successfully implemented in other schools
   (7) Provide a program best suited to the needs of the middle level age student
   (8) Move ninth graders into a high school program
   (9) Provide fifth and/or sixth graders with more curricular specialization
   (10) Does not apply.

53. Ability grouping is the assignment of students to classes based upon academic ability. Which statement best describes your opinion about academic ability grouping of students (excluding special education classes)?
   (1) There should be *no form* of ability grouping
   (2) Ability grouping of students *into certain classes* is appropriate
   (3) Ability grouping of students into any class is not appropriate, but grouping of students for instruction *within a class* is appropriate.

54. Listed below are sports often associated with middle level education. For the appropriate sports, circle the number which represents the grade level and the sex of the students *you feel* should be given the opportunity to participate in interscholastic competition (between schools). *We are interested in your opinion at all grade levels,* not only for those levels in your own building.

SPORTS	GRADE 5		GRADE 6		GRADE 7		GRADE 8		GRADE 9	
	Boys	Girls	Boys	Girls	Boys	Girls	Boys	Girls	Boys	Girls
(1) No interscholastic sports	1	2	3	4	5	6	7	8	9	0
(2) Baseball	1	2	3	4	5	6	7	8	9	0
(3) Basketball	1	2	3	4	5	6	7	8	9	0
(4) Football	1	2	3	4	5	6	7	8	9	0
(5) Gymnastics	1	2	3	4	5	6	7	8	9	0
(6) Ice Hockey	1	2	3	4	5	6	7	8	9	0
(7) Soccer	1	2	3	4	5	6	7	8	9	0
(8) Softball	1	2	3	4	5	6	7	8	9	0
(9) Swimming	1	2	3	4	5	6	7	8	9	0
(10) Tennis	1	2	3	4	5	6	7	8	9	0
(11) Track	1	2	3	4	5	6	7	8	9	0
(12) Volleyball	1	2	3	4	5	6	7	8	9	0
(13) Wrestling	1	2	3	4	5	6	7	8	9	0
(14) Other:_____	1	2	3	4	5	6	7	8	9	0

55. What forms of educational technology do you utilize in the instructional programs of your school? *Circle all that apply.*
   (1) No educational technology is used in our school
   (2) Educational television channels/programs only
   (3) Distance education (remote access combining several technologies)
   (4) Interactive video (remote access)
   (5) Interactive video (within school)
   (6) Computer-managed instruction
   (7) Computer-assisted instruction
   (8) Other:_____

56. Identify each response which represents an administrative use of computers, data processing equipment or other technological services in your school.
   (1) Scheduling classes
   (2) Preparing grade reports
   (3) Maintaining student records on attendance
   (4) Maintaining student records on disciplinary behaviors
   (5) Maintaining personnel records
   (6) Selecting samples for student or parent surveys
   (7) Interactive communication device with other professionals
   (8) Interactive communication device to identify and retrieve instructional materials
   (9) Maintaining fiscal records
   (10) Preparing written communications such as brochures and newsletters
   (11) Processing correspondence and meeting other basic office operational needs
   (12) Facilitating operations in the library/media center
   (13) Providing a hot-line information service to persons who call the school
   (14) Providing computer-based telephone messages to the home (e.g., to notify parents of student absences)
   (15) Assisting teachers in the preparation and development of tests and teaching materials
   (16) Scoring teacher-made tests
   (17) Other:_____

57. Please indicate the degree to which *you believe* the middle level characteristics listed below are important to an instructionally effective middle level school. Then, indicate the degree to which *your school currently implements* these middle level characteristics. Finally, please identify the *plans you have* in your school to implement each characteristic.

CATEGORY DESCRIPTIONS:

Importance of Characteristic. Use the following scale to describe the degree of importance of each characteristic in an instructionally effective middle level school.
(1) Little or no importance—absence of this characteristic will not affect the operation of the school.
(2) Somewhat important—presence of this characteristic adds to the quality of the school.
(3) Very important—presence of this characteristic is critical to a quality school.

Current Implementation: Use the following scale to describe the degree of implementation of each characteristic.
(1) No implementation—we do not have this characteristic in our school.
(2) Partial implementation—we implement this characteristic but not every aspect as it is described in the statement.
(3) Full implementation—we implement every aspect of the characteristic as described in the statement.

Plans for Implementation. Use the following scale to describe the plans you have in your school for implementing the characteristic.
(1) We implement the characteristic fully and plan to continue to do so.
(2) We implement the characteristic fully but plan to discontinue doing so in the next two years.
(3) We do not implement the characteristic fully but already have plans to do so in the next two years.
(4) We do not implement the characteristic fully but are considering full implementation in the next two years.
(5) We do not implement the characteristic fully and plan to continue as we are for the next two years.

CHARACTERISTIC:	Importance of Characteristic	Current Implementation	Plans for Implementation
(1) Interdisciplinary teams of 2-5 teachers sharing common students, common planning time, and housed in close proximity.	1 2 3	1 2 3	1 2 3 4 5
(2) Exploratory course offerings which provide required (not elective) curricular opportunities for all students (e.g., computers, family living, industrial technology, music).	1 2 3	1 2 3	1 2 3 4 5
(3) Adviser-advisee program regularly scheduled for 15 minutes or more during each classroom day.	1 2 3	1 2 3	1 2 3 4 5
(4) Cocurricular program separate from regular graded courses, but occurring during the school day, designed to provide students with the opportunity to pursue leadership roles, special interests, and socialization.	1 2 3	1 2 3	1 2 3 4 5
(5) Intramural activities offered for all students during or immediately after the regular classroom day.	1 2 3	1 2 3	1 2 3 4 5

58. Vertical articulation, the coordination of efforts between grade levels, is important in middle level education. Indicate the degree to which there is an articulation **problem** with either the elementary or secondary level for the issues listed below. Please respond for both elementary and secondary levels.

	Elementary Articulation			Secondary Articulation		
ISSUE	No Problem	Minor Problem	Major Problem	No Problem	Minor Problem	Major Problem
(1) Orientation of students	1	2	3	1	2	3
(2) Student grading practices	1	2	3	1	2	3
(3) Instructional delivery systems	1	2	3	1	2	3
(4) Teaching methodology	1	2	3	1	2	3
(5) Subject content and sequence	1	2	3	1	2	3
(6) Pupil promotion policies	1	2	3	1	2	3
(7) Student records	1	2	3	1	2	3
(8) Granting of subject credit	1	2	3	1	2	3
(9) Counseling services	1	2	3	1	2	3
(10) Cocurricular activities	1	2	3	1	2	3
(11) Interscholastic sports	1	2	3	1	2	3

59. In which type of professional organization do you hold local, state or national membership? *Circle all that are appropriate.*
    (1) Professional teacher association or union (e.g., NEA, AFT)
    (2) Professional administrator association or union (e.g., NASSP, NAESP)
    (3) Subject area professional association (e.g., National Council of Teachers of English)
    (4) Honorary professional association (e.g., Phi Delta Kappa)
    (5) General professional association for the middle level (e.g., National Middle School Association)
    (6) Other:_____
    (7) I do not hold membership in a professional association

60. Circle all of the following that apply to your district's support for your participation in the activities of professional educational organizations.
    (1) Discourages active participation in professional organizations
    (2) Encourages active participation in professional organizations
    (3) Pays my membership dues
    (4) Allows released time to attend meetings/conferences
    (5) Pays a portion (half or less) of my expenses to attend meetings/conferences
    (6) Pays all or most of my expenses to attend meetings/conferences

61. Circle the type of professional development activity in which you have been involved during the past two years.
    (1) National professional organization institute or conference (voluntary participation)
    (2) State professional organization activity (voluntary participation)
    (3) Activity conducted by private consultants at an out-of-district location (voluntary participation)
    (4) District activity required as part of employment
    (5) Other district activities (voluntary participation)
    (6) Enrollment in graduate courses at a college or university
    (7) State department or regional educational agency activity (voluntary participation)
    (8) State department or regional educational agency activity (required participation)
    (9) Principal center or Academy (voluntary participation)
    (10) Other: specify_____

Thank you for taking the time to complete this survey!
Please return the survey in the envelope provided.

National Association of Secondary School Principals

A National Study of Leadership in Middle Level Education

Assistant Principal Survey

Directions

Your questionnaire is identified by the label placed on it. It is not necessary to sign or place your name on the questionnaire. In reporting results, only statistical summaries of the responses for groups of respondents will be cited. In no case will identity of an individual be divulged. You are urged to make every answer a sincere one.

Circle the number of the appropriate response using pen or pencil. If you change a response, please make the change obvious so there is no doubt about how you wish to answer.

Please attempt to answer every question. For some questions none of the alternatives may correspond exactly to your situation, or to the opinion you hold. In such cases mark the alternative which comes closest to the answer you would like to give.

For the purposes of this study, two terms should be clarified:

(1) **Middle level education** is a general phrase used to encompass various combinations of grades five through nine.

(2) **Assistant principal** refers to the building administrator with the title of assistant, vice, or associate principal and should not be confused with principal, administrative intern, dean of students, etc.

> PLEASE NOTE: The member of the staff completing this questionnaire should be an "assistant principal" according to the above definition. If the school does not have an "assistant principal," this survey should not be completed.

Return your completed questionnaire to NASSP in the envelope provided. Thank you for your participation in this important study.

Please Return This Questionnaire Within 10 Days

Advisory Committee for the National Study of Leadership in Middle Level Education:
James Anding, Nathan Hale Junior High School, Omaha, NE; James Aseltine, Irving Robbins Middle School, Farmington, CT; Don Dalton, Canyon Vista Middle School, Austin, TX; Marion Payne, Owen Brown Middle School, Columbia, MD; Lori Simmons, Commodore Bainbridge Middle School, Bainbridge Island, WA; Joseph Tafoya, Santa Ana Unified School District, Santa Ana, CA; Sue Carol Thompson, Blue Valley School District, Overland Park, KS.

Research Team:
Donald Clark, University of Arizona; Judith Irvin, Florida State University; James Keefe, NASSP; George Melton, NASSP Emeritus; Jerry Valentine, University of Missouri

Demographic and Control Questions

1. What is your sex?
   (1) Male   (2) Female

2. What is your age?
   (1) 24 and under   (6) 45-49
   (2) 25-29   (7) 50-54
   (3) 30-34   (8) 55-59
   (4) 35-39   (9) 60 or older
   (5) 40-44

3. With what ethnic group would you identify your-self?
   (1) White   (4) American Indian
   (2) Black   (5) Asian
   (3) Chicano/Hispanic   (6) Other:_____

4. What is your official job title?
   (1) Assistant principal   (3) Associate principal
   (2) Vice principal   (4) Other:_____

5. At what age were you appointed to your first assistant principalship?
   (1) 24 and under   (6) 45-49
   (2) 25-29   (7) 50-54
   (3) 30-34   (8) 55-59
   (4) 35-39   (9) 60 or older
   (5) 40-44

6. How many years have you been an assistant principal in this school, including this current year?
   (1) One   (6) 9-11
   (2) Two   (7) 12-14
   (3) Three   (8) 15-17
   (4) 4-5   (9) 18 or more
   (5) 6-8

7. How many years have you served as an assistant principal, including this current year?
   (1) One   (6) 10-14
   (2) 2-3   (7) 15-19
   (3) 4-5   (8) 20-24
   (4) 6-7   (9) 25 or more
   (5) 8-9

8. How many years of teaching experience, regard-less of level, did you have prior to taking your present position? Do not include years as a full-time administrator or supervisor.
   (1) None   (6) 10-14
   (2) One   (7) 15-19
   (3) 2-3   (8) 20-24
   (4) 4-6   (9) 25 or more
   (5) 7-9

9. In which of the following areas did you major as an undergraduate? *Circle only one answer.*
   (1) Mathematics
   (2) Physical or biological sciences
   (3) Social sciences (sociology, history, etc)
   (4) Humanities (literature, languages, etc.)
   (5) Physical education
   (6) Business
   (7) Fine arts
   (8) Vocational-Technical (home economics, industrial arts, etc.)
   (9) Elementary education
   (10) Secondary education (other than physical education)
   (11) Middle level education
   (12) Other:_____

10. What is the highest degree you have earned?
    (1) Less than bachelor's
    (2) Bachelor's degree
    (3) Master's degree in education
    (4) Master's degree not in education
    (5) Master's degree plus some additional gradu-ate work
    (6) Educational Specialist, six-year program or equivalent
    (7) Master's degree plus *all coursework* for a doctorate
    (8) Doctor of Education
    (9) Doctor of Philosophy
    (10) Other:_____

11. What is your major field of *graduate study? Circle only one answer.*
    (1) Educational administration and supervision
    (2) Secondary education, curriculum and instruction
    (3) Elementary education, curriculum and instruction
    (4) Guidance and counseling
    (5) Physical education
    (6) Some other educational specialty:_____
    (7) Humanities, social sciences, or fine arts
    (8) Math or sciences
    (9) Business
    (10) Other:_____
    (11) No graduate study.

12. Which of the following *best* represents your administrative certification for the principalship or assistant principalship? *Choose only one answer.*
    (1) Secondary
    (2) Middle
    (3) Elementary
    (4) No building level certification
    (5) Other:_____

13. What is your career plan for the next 3-5 years? *Circle one.*
    (1) Remain in present position
    (2) Retirement
    (3) Seek position as superintendent
    (4) Seek a central office position other than superintendent
    (5) Seek a different position as an assistant principal at the middle level
    (6) Seek a position as an assistant principal at a different level of education
    (7) Seek a position as a middle level principal
    (8) Seek a position as a high school principal
    (9) Seek a position as an elementary principal
    (10) Seek a position in a junior college or university
    (11) Seek a position in a state department of education or other educational service agency (other than a school district)
    (12) Return to full time teaching
    (13) Seek a position in a career field other than education
    (14) I am undecided

14. What was the last position you held prior to becoming a middle level assistant principal? *Circle only one answer.*
    (1) Elementary teacher
    (2) Middle level teacher
    (3) High school teacher
    (4) Assistant principal of an elementary school
    (5) Assistant principal of a middle level school
    (6) Assistant principal of a high school
    (7) Principal of an elementary school
    (8) Principal of a middle level school
    (9) Principal of a high school
    (10) Guidance counselor
    (11) Central office administrator
    (12) College administrator or instructor
    (13) Other:_____

15. In which of the following positions have you had one full year or more of experience. *Circle all that apply.*
    (1) Athletic coach
    (2) Athletic director
    (3) Counselor or guidance position
    (4) Dean or registrar
    (5) Department chairperson
    (6) Team Leader
    (7) Dean of Studies
    (8) Dean of Students
    (9) Activities Director

16. What is your current annual salary? *Do not consider fringe benefits.*
    (1) Less than $30,000   (7) 55,000-59,999
    (2) 30,000-34,999   (8) 60,000-64,999
    (3) 35,000-39,999   (9) 65,000-69,999
    (4) 40,000-44,999   (10) 70,000 or more
    (5) 45,000-49,999   (11) Not applicable
    (6) 50,000-54,999   (religious order)

17. In addition to salary, which of the following fringe benefits do you receive from your school or district? *Circle all appropriate responses.*
    (1) No fringe benefits
    (2) Automobile mileage allowance
    (3) Retirement
    (4) Dental Insurance
    (5) Expense account
    (6) Housing or equivalent subsidy
    (7) Life insurance
    (8) Meals
    (9) Medical insurance
    (10) College tuition for yourself
    (11) Tuition for dependents (non-public)

18. What is the basis for your salary determination?
    (1) Percentage of a step in the teacher salary schedule
    (2) Teacher salary schedule plus an increment for administration
    (3) Negotiations are held for administration separate from teacher negotiations
    (4) Negotiated on an individual basis
    (5) Non-negotiated administrative salary schedule
    (6) Does not apply (e.g., religious order)
    (7) Other:_____

19. Regardless of payment schedule, on what time period is your yearly salary contract based?
    (1) 12 months   (5) 10
    (2) 11½   (6) 9½
    (3) 11   (7) 9
    (4) 10½

20. Is your contract multi-year?
    (1) No
    (2) Yes—two year contract
    (3) Yes—three year contract
    (4) Yes—more than three year contract

21. Do you have *tenure as an assistant principal?*
    (1) Yes   (2) No

22. Which of the following categories best describes the middle level school of which you are an assistant principal. *Select only one.*
    (1) Public
    (2) Parochial or diocesan
    (3) Private, religious affiliated
    (4) Private, not religious affiliated
    (5) Other:_____

23. How many students are currently enrolled in your school?
    (1) Less than 200   (7) 1200-1399
    (2) 200-399   (8) 1400-1599
    (3) 400-599   (9) 1600-1799
    (4) 600-799   (10) 1800-1999
    (5) 800-999   (11) 2000 or more
    (6) 1000-1199

24. What grades are included in the middle level school of which you are an assistant principal?
    (1) 7-8-9   (6) 5-6
    (2) 6-7-8   (7) 6-7
    (3) 5-6-7   (8) 7-8
    (4) 5-6-7-8   (9) 8-9
    (5) 6-7-8-9   (10) Other:_____

25. Which of the following population categories best describes the locality of the middle level school of which you are an assistant principal?
    (1) City, more than 1,000,000
    (2) City, 150,000 to 999,999
    (3) Suburban, related to city of 150,000 population or more
    (4) City, 25,000 to 149, 999 population, distinct from a metropolitan area
    (5) City, 5,000 to 24,999, not suburban
    (6) Town or rural under 4,999

26. In which geographical region is your school located?
    (1) New England   (5) Southwest
    (2) Mid-Atlantic   (6) Rocky Mountain
    (3) South   (7) West Coast
    (4) Midwest   (8) Alaska or Hawaii

School Leadership Questions

27. During the school year, on the average, how many hours a week do you work at your job as assistant principal?
    (1) Less than 40   (4) 60-69
    (2) 40-49   (5) 70 or more
    (3) 50-59

28. Do you have a written job description for your position as assistant principal?
    (1) Yes   (2) No

29. Do you teach any regularly scheduled classes?
    (1) No   (3) Yes—two or more
    (2) Yes—one course   courses

30. How many assistant principals are there in your school? (Include yourself.)
    (1) One—part time   (3) Two
    (2) One—full time   (4) Three or More
    (5) None—but I hold an equivalent position

31. How many female assistant principals are there in your school? (Include yourself if applicable.)
    (1) One   (3) Three or more
    (2) Two   (4) None

32. Who assigns the duties and responsibilities of the leadership team?
    (1) Principal alone
    (2) Superintendent alone
    (3) School board alone
    (4) Principal in conference with assistant principal
    (5) Principal in conference with assistant principal and others
    (6) Principal and superintendent or school board
    (7) Other:_____

33. How do you spend your time during the typical work week? Rank these nine areas according to the amount of time spent in each area. In Column A, *mark a "1" next to the area in which you* do spend *the most time, ranking all areas until you have marked a "9" next to the area in which you spend the least time.* Then in Column B, *mark a "1" next to the area in which you feel you* should spend *the most time, ranking all items accordingly until you have marked "9" next to the area in which you feel you should spend the least time.*

A. *Do Spend Time*	Area of Responsibility	B. *Should Spend Time*
_____	(1) *Community* (PTA, advisory groups, parent conferences, etc.)	_____
_____	(2) *District Office* (meetings, task forces, reports, etc.)	_____
_____	(3) *Personnel* (evaluating, advising, conferring, recruiting, etc.)	_____
_____	(4) *Planning* (annual, long range)	_____
_____	(5) *Professional Development* (reading, conferences, etc.)	_____
_____	(6) *Program Development* (curriculum, instructional leadership, etc.)	_____
_____	(7) *School Management* (weekly calendar, office, budget, memos, etc.)	_____
_____	(8) *Student Activities* (meetings, supervision, planning, etc.)	_____
_____	(9) *Student Behavior* (discipline, attendance, meetings, etc.)	_____

The next two questions are about "leadership teams." Please respond according to the following definition of a "leadership team." A **Leadership team** is a group of teachers and administrators designated by the principal or elected by the faculty to assist in the leadership operation of the school. These staff members may have been formally designated, or they may be a more informal group obviously instrumental in the on-going operation of the school. If you do not have a leadership team, mark the box below and go to question 36.

☐ We do not have a leadership team in our school.

34. How many people on your staff comprise your "leadership team?"

(1) One
(2) Two
(3) Three
(4) Four
(5) Five
(6) Six
(7) Seven
(8) More than 7

35. What are the job position titles of persons on your "leadership team?" *Circle all that apply.*

(1) teacher
(2) dean
(3) assistant principal
(4) administrative intern
(5) counselor
(6) coordinator
(7) director
(8) team leader
(9) Other:_____

36. Various individuals or groups are important to the decision-making process at the building level. Consider the types of decisions in the left-hand column and then indicate the degree of involvement of each person(s) in the appropriate box. *Mark a "1"* in the cell to indicate those who discuss the decision; *Mark a "2"* for those who make recommendations; *Mark a "3"* for those who make the actual decision; *Mark a "0"* if there is no involvement.

Thus: 0 = *No involvement*   2 = *Make recommendations*
         1 = *Involved in discussion*   3 = *Make decision*

	Principal	Assistant Principal	Leadership Team	Team Ldrs. Dept. Chairs	Staff Committees	Faculty as a Whole	Individual Teacher	Students	Parents/ Community	Central Office	School Board
(1) Adding a new course or instructional program											
(2) Adopting rules for student behavior											
(3) Curricular reform											
(4) Developing a budget for your school											
(5) Evaluating teaching staff											
(6) Evaluating the school's grading practices											
(7) Formulating school goals & mission											
(8) Hiring teaching staff											
(9) School organization (teams vs. depts.)											

37. **Duties and responsibilities of Assistant Principals.** Principals have final responsibility for everything that happens in a school, but assistant principals share in differing degrees in that responsibility. Please describe *your* job profile using the alternatives listed below.

Responsibility. Please circle the number which indicates the degree of responsibility you have for each job function. Use the following scale:
(1) Minor Responsibility—Principal does the job; I may provide assistance at principal's discretion.
(2) Moderate Responsibility—The job is delegated but is closely supervised; principal and I work together.
(3) Major Responsibility—The job is delegated and not closely supervised; I am held responsible for the job.

Importance. Please circle the number which indicates the degree of importance the delegated duty has to the effective functioning of the school. Use the following scale:
(1) Minor importance—The job is not very important. If it is not completed effectively, there will not be a significant negative effect on overall school effectiveness.
(2) Moderate importance—The job is important. If it is not completed effectively, the overall effectiveness of the school is diminished.
(3) Major importance—The job is critical. If it is not completed effectively, the overall effectiveness of the school is significantly impaired.

Degree of Discretionary Behavior. Please circle the number which indicates the degree of discretionary behavior associated with the job function. Use the following scale:
(1) Minor discretionary behavior—The behavior needed to complete the function is almost completely dictated by others; I make few, if any, decisions.
(2) Moderate discretionary behavior—The behavior needed to complete the function is generally self-directing, with little direction from others. I have the opportunity to make most decisions associated with this function.
(3) Major discretionary behavior—The behavior needed to complete the function is completely self-directing. I receive no direction from others and make all decisions associated with this function.

Not Applicable. Please circle the "0" for any job function that does not apply to you.

DUTIES:	Not Applicable	Responsibility			Importance			Discretionary Behavior		
		Minor	Moderate	Major	Minor	Moderate	Major	Minor	Moderate	Major
(1) Adviser/Advisee Program	0	1	2	3	1	2	3	1	2	3
(2) Articulation with Elementary School	0	1	2	3	1	2	3	1	2	3
(3) Articulation with High School	0	1	2	3	1	2	3	1	2	3
(4) Building Use/Calendar	0	1	2	3	1	2	3	1	2	3
(5) Community Relations	0	1	2	3	1	2	3	1	2	3
(6) Cocurricular Activities	0	1	2	3	1	2	3	1	2	3
(7) Curriculum	0	1	2	3	1	2	3	1	2	3
(8) Department Teams	0	1	2	3	1	2	3	1	2	3
(9) Discipline/Attendance	0	1	2	3	1	2	3	1	2	3
(10) Guidance/Health Service	0	1	2	3	1	2	3	1	2	3
(11) Instructional Improvement	0	1	2	3	1	2	3	1	2	3
(12) Instructional Materials	0	1	2	3	1	2	3	1	2	3
(13) Interdisciplinary Teams	0	1	2	3	1	2	3	1	2	3
(14) Interscholastic Athletics	0	1	2	3	1	2	3	1	2	3
(15) Parental Involvement/Volunteers	0	1	2	3	1	2	3	1	2	3
(16) Scheduling	0	1	2	3	1	2	3	1	2	3
(17) School Goal Setting	0	1	2	3	1	2	3	1	2	3
(18) Staff Development	0	1	2	3	1	2	3	1	2	3
(19) Support/Non-instructional Staff	0	1	2	3	1	2	3	1	2	3
(20) Transportation	0	1	2	3	1	2	3	1	2	3

38. For the next question, circle the number which describes your perception of how your job actually is; then for the following question, circle the number which describes how you think your job should be.
How much prestige do you feel your position as a member of the leadership team *provides*?

1	2	3	4	5
Little		Moderate		Much

How much prestige do you feel your position as a member of the leadership team *should provide*?

1	2	3	4	5
Little		Moderate		Much

39. If you could choose again, would you select education as a career?
   (1) Yes—definitely   (4) No—probably not
   (2) Yes—probably   (5) No—definitely not
   (3) Uncertain

40. At what career point did you decide to enter educational administration?
   (1) About the same time I decided to enter the educational profession
   (2) After my first few years in the profession
   (3) After considerable experience in the profession (5 years or more)

41. Rate the influence that the following groups or individuals had on your decision to enter educational administration.

	Little or No Influence	Moderate Influence	Great Influence	Unsure or Don't Know
(1) Parents	1	2	3	0
(2) Spouse	1	2	3	0
(3) Colleagues	1	2	3	0
(4) Professors	1	2	3	0
(5) School administrator	1	2	3	0
(6) Other_____	1	2	3	0

42. Which of the following is most descriptive of the position held by the person who most directly influenced your ability to function effectively during your initial year as an assistant principal?
   (1) Another assistant principal
   (2) A principal
   (3) A professor
   (4) A teacher(s)
   (5) A central office administrator
   (6) Other:_____
   (7) No one person was particularly influential

43. How **important** to you were the following statements about jobs and careers at the time that you decided to: (a) enter teaching? and (b) enter administration?

Teaching or Administration will:	A. TEACHING			B. ADMINISTRATION		
	Little/No Importance	Somewhat Important	Very Important	Little/No Importance	Somewhat Important	Very Important
(1) Provide an opportunity to make a good salary	1	2	3	1	2	3
(2) Provide an opportunity to use my special abilities and aptitudes	1	2	3	1	2	3
(3) Provide social status and prestige	1	2	3	1	2	3
(4) Provide opportunity to work with people rather than things	1	2	3	1	2	3
(5) Permit me to be creative and original	1	2	3	1	2	3
(6) Provide an opportunity to exercise leadership	1	2	3	1	2	3
(7) Provide a stable and secure future	1	2	3	1	2	3
(8) Provide the opportunity to be helpful to others	1	2	3	1	2	3
(9) Offer excellent hours and vacations	1	2	3	1	2	3
(10) Provide an opportunity to help students	1	2	3	1	2	3
(11) Offer recognition by others	1	2	3	1	2	3
(12) Provide opportunity to improve curriculum and instruction	1	2	3	1	2	3
(13) Other:_____	1	2	3	1	2	3

44. Rate the following as they contributed to your preparation as an assistant principal.

	None	Little or Moderate	Great	Never Held
(1) Work as a teacher	1	2	3	0
(2) Work as an adviser of a student activity	1	2	3	0
(3) Work as a guidance counselor	1	2	3	0
(4) Work as a department head or team leader	1	2	3	0
(5) Work as a member of a school leadership team	1	2	3	0
(6) Participation in community activities	1	2	3	0
(7) Participation in professional activities	1	2	3	0
(8) University coursework	1	2	3	0
(9) University field experiences	1	2	3	0

45. What is your perception of the importance of the following items as they contributed to your first appointment to the assistant principalship?

	Little or No Importance	Somewhat Important	Very Important
(1) Amount and quality of professional preparation	1	2	3
(2) Assessment Center report	1	2	3
(3) Contacts outside the profession	1	2	3
(4) Contacts within the profession	1	2	3
(5) I was at the right spot at the right time	1	2	3
(6) Number of years of teaching experience	1	2	3
(7) Performance in formal assignments outside the classroom (e.g., department head, team leader, coach, sponsor)	1	2	3
(8) Performance in informal assignments outside the classroom (e.g., assembly program chair, faculty social)	1	2	3
(9) Performance on competitive exams	1	2	3
(10) Success as a teacher	1	2	3
(11) Success as a counselor, librarian, etc.	1	2	3
(12) Successful job interview	1	2	3
(13) The principal wanted me	1	2	3
(14) The superintendent or assistant superintendent wanted me	1	2	3
(15) Other:_____	1	2	3

46. To what extent did the following individuals affect the final decision by which you were appointed assistant principal?

	Little or No Influence	Moderate Influence	Great Influence
(1) Principal of the school	1	2	3
(2) Superintendent of the district	1	2	3
(3) Board of Education	1	2	3
(4) University Professor	1	2	3
(5) Other professional contacts	1	2	3
(6) Friends	1	2	3
(7) Other:_____	1	2	3

47. To what degree have the circumstances listed below affected your decisions to change or not change school districts?

	Little or No Influence	Moderate Influence	Great Influence
(1) Family commitment (i.e. children, relatives) motivated me to pass up or not seek opportunities in other districts.	1	2	3
(2) Desire to live in a certain part of the country made me more place-oriented than career-oriented.	1	2	3
(3) The school environment (e.g., student discipline, parental views) has always been an important factor in my selection of jobs.	1	2	3
(4) Commitment to the middle level of education has caused me to remain at this level rather than change positions.	1	2	3
(5) Job security, seniority and retirements benefits outweigh the advantages that might ensue from changing school districts.	1	2	3
(6) Other:_____	1	2	3

48. Please rate your degree of job satisfaction with your job environment as assistant principal.

Satisfaction with:	Dissatisfied	Satisfied	Very Satisfied	Unsure
(1) The realization of expectations you had when you took the job	1	2	3	0
(2) The amount of time you devote to the job	1	2	3	0
(3) The results that you achieve	1	2	3	0
(4) The salary you receive	1	2	3	0
(5) The working conditions	1	2	3	0
(6) The amount of assistance you receive from your immediate supervisor	1	2	3	0
(7) The rapport you have with your supervisor	1	2	3	0
(8) The rapport you have with your administrative colleagues	1	2	3	0
(9) The rapport you have with teachers	1	2	3	0
(10) The rapport you have with students	1	2	3	0
(11) The rapport you have with parents and members of the community	1	2	3	0

Issues and Trends Questions

49. What do you think is the ideal grade organizational structure for the middle level school?
(1) 7-8-9
(2) 6-7-8
(3) 5-6-7
(4) 5-6-7-8
(5) 6-7-8-9
(6) 5-6
(7) 6-7
(8) 7-8
(9) 8-9
(10) Other:_____

50. All things considered (learning conditions, teaching staff, capital outlay, etc.), what is your judgment about the optimum number of students for a middle level school?
(1) Less than 200
(2) 200-399
(3) 400-599
(4) 600-799
(5) 800-999
(6) 1000-1199
(7) 1200-1399
(8) 1400-1599
(9) 1600-1799
(10) 1800-1999
(11) 2000 or more

51. Ability grouping is the assignment of students to classes based upon academic ability. Which statement best describes your opinion about ability grouping of students (excluding special education classes).
    (1) There should be *no form* of ability grouping.
    (2) Ability grouping of students *into certain classes* is appropriate.
    (3) Ability grouping of students into any class is not appropriate, but grouping of students for instruction *within a class* is appropriate.

52. Identify any grade levels at which you feel greater emphasis should be placed upon intramural rather than interscholastic activities.
    (1) All middle level grades
    (2) Grades 8 and below
    (3) Grades 7 and below
    (4) Grades 6 and below
    (5) Grade 5

53. In recent years technological advancements (e.g., satellite communication, instructional television, computer-assisted instruction) have provided schools with opportunities for instructional methods not used 10 to 20 years ago. Do you believe educational technology *has improved* the quality of the learning experiences for students in your school?
    (1) Yes   (2) No

54. Do you believe educational technology *will improve* the quality of educational instruction for future students in your school?
    (1) Yes   (2) No

55. Using the following scale, please indicate the degree to which you believe the middle level characteristics listed below are important to an instructionally effective middle level school.
    (1) Little or no importance—absence of this characteristic will not affect the operation of the school.
    (2) Somewhat important—presence of this characteristic adds to the quality of the school.
    (3) Very important—presence of this characteristic is critical to a quality school.

Characteristic	Little or No Importance	Somewhat Important	Very Important
(1) Interdisciplinary teams of 2-5 teachers sharing common students, common planning time, and housed in close proximity.	1	2	3
(2) Exploratory course offerings which provide required (not elective) curricular opportunities for all students, e.g., computers, family living, industrial technology, music.	1	2	3
(3) Adviser-advisee program regularly scheduled for 15 minutes or more during each classroom day.	1	2	3
(4) Cocurricular program separate from regular graded courses, but occurring during the school day, designed to provide students with the opportunity to pursue leadership roles, special interests, and socialization.	1	2	3
(5) Intramural activities offered for all students during or immediately after the regular classroom day.	1	2	3

56. Listed below are several factors which could be considered "roadblocks" preventing assistant principals from doing the job they would like to do. Indicate the degree to which each factor has or has not been a roadblock to you as assistant principal over the past two years.

FACTOR	Not a Factor	Moderate Factor	Serious Factor
(1) Collective bargaining agreement	1	2	3
(2) Deficient communication among administrative levels	1	2	3
(3) Inability to obtain funding	1	2	3
(4) Inability to provide teacher time for planning or professional development	1	2	3
(5) Insufficient space and physical facilities	1	2	3

(6) Lack of competent administrative assistance	1	2	3
(7) Lack of competent office help	1	2	3
(8) Lack of data about student skills and styles	1	2	3
(9) Lack of data on program successes/failures	1	2	3
(10) Lack of district-wide flexibility (all schools conform to same policy)	1	2	3
(11) Lack of knowledge among staff regarding programs for middle level students	1	2	3
(12) Lack of time for myself	1	2	3
(13) Long-standing tradition in the school/district	1	2	3
(14) Parents apathetic or irresponsible about their children	1	2	3
(15) Pressure from community	1	2	3
(16) Problem students (apathetic, hostile, etc.)	1	2	3
(17) Regulations or mandates from state or district governing boards	1	2	3
(18) Resistance to change by staff	1	2	3
(19) Superintendent or central office staff	1	2	3
(20) Teacher tenure	1	2	3
(21) Teacher turnover	1	2	3
(22) Time required to administer/supervise extracurricular activities	1	2	3
(23) Time taken by administrative detail at expense of more important matters	1	2	3
(24) Too large a student body	1	2	3
(25) Too small a student body	1	2	3
(26) Variations in the ability and dedication of staff	1	2	3

57. In which type of professional organization do you hold local, state, or national membership?
    (1) Professional teacher association or union; e.g., NEA, AFT
    (2) Professional administrator association or union; e.g., NASSP, NAESP
    (3) Subject area professional association; e.g., National Council of Teachers of English.
    (4) Honorary professional association; e.g., Phi Delta Kappa
    (5) General professional association for the middle level; e.g., National Middle School Association
    (6) Other:_____
    (7) I do not hold membership in a professional association.

58. Mark all of the following that apply to your district's support for your participation in the activities of professional educational organizations
    (1) Discourages active participation in professional organizations
    (2) Encourages active participation in professional organizations
    (3) Pays my membership dues
    (4) Allows released time to attend meetings/conferences
    (5) Pays a portion (half or less) of my expenses to attend meetings/conferences
    (6) Pays all or most of my expenses to attend meetings/conferences

59. Circle the type of professional development activity in which you have been involved during the past two years.
    (1) National professional organization institute or conference (voluntary participation)
    (2) State professional organization activity (voluntary participation)
    (3) Activity conducted by private consultants at an out-of-district location (voluntary participation)
    (4) District activity required as part of employment
    (5) Other district activities (voluntary participation)
    (6) Enrollment in graduate courses at a college or university
    (7) State department or regional educational agency activity (voluntary participation)
    (8) State department or regional educational agency activity (required participation)
    (9) Principal center or academy (voluntary participation)
    (10) Other:_____

60. Please identify the *three* most important skills/characteristics of an "excellent" middle level teacher. *Circle only three.*
    (1) Competence in subject matter knowledge
    (2) Competence in use of varied methods of instruction
    (3) Competence in adjusting instruction to the varying learning styles and learning skills of the students
    (4) Competence in developing a positive relationship with students in the classroom
    (5) Competence in counseling students
    (6) Competence in working as a team member
    (7) Competence in using positive methods for student discipline
    (8) Competence in promoting positive student self-concept
    (9) Competence in employee behaviors and work habits (dependability, punctuality, attendance)
    (10) Competence in working with parents
    (11) Competence in working with colleagues

61. Much has been written about the tasks of American schools. Please rank the 11 statements below according to *your belief* about their relative importance as educational purposes.

    Assign a rank of "1" to the statement you consider most important, a rank of "2" to the next most important, until you assign a rank of "11" to the statement you consider least important.

    ____ (1) Acquisition of basic skills (reading, writing, speaking, computing, etc.)
    ____ (2) Appreciation for and experience with the fine arts
    ____ (3) Career planning and training in beginning occupational skills
    ____ (4) Development of moral and spiritual values
    ____ (5) Development of positive self-concept and good human relations
    ____ (6) Development of skills and practice in critical intellectual inquiry and problem solving
    ____ (7) Development of the skills to operate a technological society (engineering, scientific, etc.)
    ____ (8) Knowledge about and skills in preparation for family life (sex education, home management, problems of aging, etc.)
    ____ (9) Preparation for a changing world
    ____ (10) Physical fitness and useful leisure time sports
    ____ (11) Understanding of the American value system (its political, economic, social values, etc.)

**Thank you for taking the time to complete this survey!
Please return the survey in the envelope provided.**

National Association of Secondary School Principals

A National Study of Leadership In Middle Level Education

Leadership Team Member Survey

Directions

Your questionnaire is identified by the label placed on it. It is not necessary to sign or place your name on the questionnaire. In reporting results, only statistical summaries of the responses for groups of respondents will be cited. In no case will the identity of an individual be divulged. You are urged to make every answer a sincere one.

Circle the number of the appropriate response using pen or pencil. If you change a response, please make the change obvious so there is no doubt about how you wish to answer.

Please attempt to answer every question. For some questions none of the alternatives may correspond exactly to your situation, or to the opinion you hold. In such cases mark the alternative which comes closest to the answer you would like to give.

For the purposes of this study, two terms should be clarified:

(1) **Middle level education** is a general phrase used to encompass various combinations of grades five through nine.

(2) **Leadership team member** is a teacher who has been designated by the principal to assist in the leadership operation of the school. If the school has a group of educators who have been formally designated as the "leadership team," the person completing this questionnaire should be a member of that group. If the school does not have a formal "leadership team," the person completing this survey should be a teacher who is instrumental in the on-going operation of the school; i.e., one who informally provides significant positive leadership for the school.

> PLEASE NOTE: The member of the faculty completing this questionnaire should be a member of the "leadership team" according to the above definition. If the school does not have a formal or informal "leadership team" this survey should not be completed.

Return your completed questionnaire to NASSP in the envelope provided. Thank you for your participation in this important study.

Please Return This Questionnaire Within 10 Days

Advisory Committee for the National Study of Leadership in Middle Level Education:
James Anding, Nathan Hale Junior High School, Omaha, NE; James Aseltine, Irving Robbins Middle School, Farmington, CT; Don Dalton, Canyon Vista Middle School, Austin, TX; Marion Payne, Owen Brown Middle School, Columbia, MD; Lori Simmons, Commodore Bainbridge Middle School, Bainbridge Island, WA; Joseph Tafoya, Santa Ana Unified School District, Santa Ana, CA; Sue Carol Thompson, Blue Valley School District, Overland Park, KS.

Research Team:
Donald Clark, University of Arizona; Judith Irvin, Florida State University; James Keefe, NASSP; George Melton, NASSP Emeritus; Jerry Valentine, University of Missouri

Demographic and Control Questions

1. What is your sex?
   (1) Male   (2) Female

2. What is your age?
   (1) 24 and under   (6) 45-49
   (2) 25-29   (7) 50-54
   (3) 30-34   (8) 55-59
   (4) 35-39   (9) 60 or older
   (5) 40-44

3. With what ethnic group would you identify yourself?
   (1) White   (4) American Indian
   (2) Black   (5) Asian
   (3) Chicano/Hispanic (6) Other:_____

4. What is your official job title?
   (1) Teacher   (5) Master Teacher
   (2) Department Chair   (6) House Leader
   (3) Team Leader   (7) Dean
   (4) Administrative   (8) Coordinator
       Intern   (9) Other:_____

5. How many years have you worked as an educator in this school, including this current year?
   (1) One   (6) 9-11
   (2) Two   (7) 12-14
   (3) Three   (8) 15-17
   (4) 4-5   (9) 18 or more
   (5) 6-8

6. How many years have you served as a teacher, including this current year?
   (1) One   (6) 10-14
   (2) 2-3   (7) 15-19
   (3) 4-5   (8) 20-24
   (4) 6-7   (9) 25 or more
   (5) 8-9

7. How many years had you taught before beginning to contribute to the operation of this school in a manner that enabled you to fit the description above as a member of the "leadership team?"
   (1) None   (6) 10-14
   (2) One   (7) 15-19
   (3) 2-3   (8) 20-24
   (4) 4-6   (9) 25 or more
   (5) 7-9

8. For how many years have you contributed to the operation of this school in a manner that enabled you to fit the description above as a member of the "leadership team?"
   (1) One   (6) 10-14
   (2) 2-3   (7) 15-19
   (3) 4-5   (8) 20-24
   (4) 6-7   (9) 25 or more
   (5) 8-9

9. Which of the following best describes your teaching area? *Circle only one answer.*
   (1) Mathematics
   (2) Physical or biological sciences
   (3) Social sciences (sociology, history, etc)
   (4) Humanities (literature, languages, etc.)
   (5) Physical education
   (6) Business
   (7) Fine arts
   (8) Vocational-Technical (home economics, industrial arts, etc.)
   (9) Elementary education
   (10) Other:_____

10. What is the highest degree you have earned?
   (1) Less than a bachelor's
   (2) Bachelor's degree
   (3) Master's degree in education
   (4) Master's degree not in education
   (5) Master's degree plus some additional graduate work
   (6) Educational Specialist, six-year program or equivalent
   (7) Master's degree plus *all coursework* for a doctorate
   (8) Doctor of Education
   (9) Doctor of Philosophy
   (10) Other:_____

11. What is your career plan for the next 3-5 years? *Circle one.*
   (1) Remain in present position
   (2) Retirement
   (3) Seek position as a building principal or assistant principal
   (4) Seek a central office position
   (5) Seek a different teaching position at the middle level
   (6) Seek a different teaching position at another grade level
   (7) Seek a position in a junior college or university

(8) Seek a position in a state department of education or other educational service agency (other than a school district)

(9) Seek a position in a career field other than education

(10) I am undecided

(11) Other:_____

12. What is the length of your contract?
   (1) 12 months   (5) 10
   (2) 11½   (7) 9
   (3) 11   (6) 9½
   (4) 10½

13. Do you receive extra pay for your role as a member of the leadership team?
   (1) Yes   (2) No

14. Which of the following categories best describes the middle level school in which you work? *Circle only one.*
   (1) Public
   (2) Parochial or diocesan
   (3) Private, religious affiliated
   (4) Private, not religious affiliated
   (5) Other:_____

15. How many students are currently enrolled in your school?
   (1) Less than 200   (7) 1200-1399
   (2) 200-399   (8) 1400-1599
   (3) 400-599   (9) 1600-1799
   (4) 600-799   (10) 1800-1999
   (5) 800-999   (11) 2000 or more
   (6) 1000-1199

16. What grades are included in the middle level school of which you are a leader?
   (1) 7-8-9   (6) 5-6
   (2) 6-7-8   (7) 6-7
   (3) 5-6-7   (8) 7-8
   (4) 5-6-7-8   (9) 8-9
   (5) 6-7-8-9   (10) Other:_____

17. Which of the following population categories best describes the locality of the middle level school of which you are a leader?
   (1) City, more than 1,000,000
   (2) City, 150,000 to 999,999
   (3) Suburban, related to city of 150,000 population or more
   (4) City, 25,000 to 149,999 population, distinct from a metropolitan area
   (5) City, 5000 to 24,999, not suburban
   (6) Town or rural under 4,999

18. In which geographical region is your school located?
   (1) New England   (5) Southwest
   (2) Mid-Atlantic   (6) Rocky Mountain
   (3) South   (7) West Coast
   (4) Midwest   (8) Alaska or Hawaii

School Leadership Questions

19. During the school year, on the average, how many hours a week do you work at your job?
   (1) Less than 40   (4) 60-69
   (2) 40-49   (5) 70 or more
   (3) 50-59

20. Do you have a written job description for your role as a member of the leadership team?
   (1) Yes   (2) No

21. Do you teach any regularly scheduled classes?
   (1) No
   (2) Yes—one or two courses
   (3) Yes—three or four courses
   (4) Yes—more than four courses

22. By giving this survey to you, your principal has indicated that he/she believes you are a part of a leadership team which plays an important role in the governance of this school. Do you believe you are a part of a leadership team at this school?
   (1) Yes—in a formal way through job title and responsibilities
   (2) Yes—in an informal way without a formal job title and responsibilities
   (3) No

23. How many people on your staff comprise your "leadership team?"
   (1) One   (5) Five
   (2) Two   (6) Six
   (3) Three   (7) Seven
   (4) Four   (8) More than 7

24. What are the job position titles of persons on your "leadership team?" *Circle all that apply.*
   - (1) Teacher
   - (2) Dean
   - (3) Assistant principal
   - (4) Administrative intern
   - (5) Counselor
   - (6) Coordinator
   - (7) Director
   - (8) Team leader
   - (9) Other:_____

25. How many females are there on your leadership team? (Include yourself if applicable.)
   - (1) One
   - (2) Two
   - (3) Three
   - (4) Four
   - (5) Five
   - (6) Six
   - (7) Seven
   - (8) More than 7

26. Who assigns the duties and responsibilities of the leadership team?
   - (1) Principal
   - (2) Principal and assistant principal(s)
   - (3) Principal and/or assistant principal in conference with the members of the leadership team
   - (4) Other:_____

27. Various individuals or groups are important to the decision-making process at the building level. Consider the types of decisions in the left-hand column and then indicate the degree of involvement of each person(s) in the appropriate box. *Mark a "1"* in the cell to indicate those who discuss the decision; *Mark a "2"* for those who make recommendations; *Mark a "3"* for those who make the actual decision; *Mark a "0"* if there is no involvement.

   Thus: 0 = *No involvement*   2 = *Make recommendations*
            1 = *Involved in discussion*   3 = *Make decision*

	Principal	Assistant Principal	Leadership Team	Team Ldrs. Dept. Chairs	Staff Committees	Faculty as a Whole	Individual Teacher	Students	Parents/ Community	Central Office	School Board
(1) Adding a new course or instructional program											
(2) Adopting rules for student behavior											
(3) Curricular reform											
(4) Developing a budget for your school											
(5) Evaluating teaching staff											
(6) Evaluating the school's grading practices											
(7) Formulating school goals & mission											
(8) Hiring teaching staff											
(9) School organization (teams vs. depts.)											

28. **Duties and responsibilities of leadership team members.** Principals have final responsibility for everything that happens in a school, but others share in differing degrees in that responsibility. Please describe *your* job profile using the alternatives listed below.

   Responsibility. Please circle the number which indicates the degree of responsibility you have for each job function. Use the following scale:
   - (1) Minor Responsibility—Principal does the job; I may provide assistance at principal's discretion.
   - (2) Moderate Responsibility—The job is delegated but is closely supervised; principal and I work together.
   - (3) Major Responsibility—The job is delegated and not closely supervised; I am held responsible for the job.

Importance. Please circle the number which indicates the degree of importance the delegated duty has to the effective functioning of the school. Use the following scale:

(1) Minor importance—The job is not very important. If it is not completed effectively, there will not be a significant negative effect on overall school effectiveness.

(2) Moderate importance—The job is important. If it is not completed effectively, the overall effectiveness of the school is diminished.

(3) Major importance—The job is critical. If it is not completed effectively, the overall effectiveness of the school is significantly impaired.

Degree of Discretionary Behavior. Please circle the number which indicates the degree of discretionary behavior associated with the job function. Use the following scale:

(1) Minor discretionary behavior—The behavior needed to complete the function is almost completely dictated by others; I make few, if any, decisions.

(2) Moderate discretionary behavior—The behavior needed to complete the function is generally self-directing, with little direction from others. I have the opportunity to make most decisions associated with this function.

(3) Major discretionary behavior—The behavior needed to complete the function is completely self-directing. I receive no direction from others and make all decisions associated with this function.

Not Applicable. Please circle the "0" for any job function that does not apply to you.

DUTIES:	Not Applicable	Responsibility Minor	Responsibility Moderate	Responsibility Major	Importance Minor	Importance Moderate	Importance Major	Discretionary Behavior Minor	Discretionary Behavior Moderate	Discretionary Behavior Major
(1) Adviser/Advisee Program	0	1	2	3	1	2	3	1	2	3
(2) Articulation with Elementary School	0	1	2	3	1	2	3	1	2	3
(3) Articulation with High School	0	1	2	3	1	2	3	1	2	3
(4) Building Use/Calendar	0	1	2	3	1	2	3	1	2	3
(5) Community Relations	0	1	2	3	1	2	3	1	2	3
(6) Cocurricular Activities	0	1	2	3	1	2	3	1	2	3
(7) Curriculum	0	1	2	3	1	2	3	1	2	3
(8) Department Teams	0	1	2	3	1	2	3	1	2	3
(9) Discipline/Attendance	0	1	2	3	1	2	3	1	2	3
(10) Guidance/Health Service	0	1	2	3	1	2	3	1	2	3
(11) Instructional Improvement	0	1	2	3	1	2	3	1	2	3
(12) Instructional Materials	0	1	2	3	1	2	3	1	2	3
(13) Interdisciplinary Teams	0	1	2	3	1	2	3	1	2	3
(14) Interscholastic Athletics	0	1	2	3	1	2	3	1	2	3
(15) Parental Involvement/Volunteers	0	1	2	3	1	2	3	1	2	3
(16) Scheduling	0	1	2	3	1	2	3	1	2	3
(17) School Goal Setting	0	1	2	3	1	2	3	1	2	3
(18) Staff Development	0	1	2	3	1	2	3	1	2	3
(19) Support/Non-instructional Staff	0	1	2	3	1	2	3	1	2	3
(20) Transportation	0	1	2	3	1	2	3	1	2	3

29. For the next question, circle the number which describes your perception of how your job actually *is*; then for the following question, circle the number which describes how you think your job *should be*.

How much prestige do you feel your position as a member of the leadership team *provides*?

1	2	3	4	5
Little		Moderate		Much

How much prestige do you feel your position as a member of the leadership team *should provide*?

1	2	3	4	5
Little		Moderate		Much

30. If you could choose again, would you select education as a career?

(1) Yes—definitely   (4) No—probably not
(2) Yes—probably   (5) No—definitely not
(3) Uncertain

31. Rate the influence that the following groups or individuals had on your decision to enter education.

	Little or No Influence	Moderate Influence	Great Influence	Unsure or Don't Know
(1) Parents	1	2	3	0
(2) Spouse	1	2	3	0
(3) Colleagues	1	2	3	0
(4) Professors	1	2	3	0
(5) School administrator	1	2	3	0
(6) Other_____	1	2	3	0

32. To what degree have the circumstances listed below affected your decisions to change or not change school districts?

	Little or No Influence	Moderate Influence	Great Influence
(1) Family commitment (i.e., children, relatives) motivated me to pass up or not seek opportunities in other districts.	1	2	3
(2) Desire to live in certain part of the country made me more place-oriented than career-oriented.	1	2	3
(3) The school environment (e.g., student discipline, parental views) has always been an important factor in my selection of jobs.	1	2	3
(4) Commitment to the middle level of education has caused me to remain at this level rather than change positions.	1	2	3
(5) Job security, seniority, and retirements benefits outweigh the advantages that might ensue from changing school districts.	1	2	3
(6) Other:_____	1	2	3

33. Please rate your degree of satisfaction with your job environment.

Satisfaction with:	Dissatisfied	Satisfied	Very Satisfied	Unsure
(1) The realization of expectations you had when you took the job	1	2	3	0
(2) The amount of time you devote to the job	1	2	3	0
(3) The results that you achieve	1	2	3	0
(4) The salary you receive	1	2	3	0
(5) The working conditions	1	2	3	0
(6) The amount of assistance you receive from your immediate supervisor	1	2	3	0
(7) The rapport you have with your supervisor	1	2	3	0
(8) The rapport you have with your administrative colleagues	1	2	3	0
(9) The rapport you have with teachers	1	2	3	0
(10) The rapport you have with students	1	2	3	0
(11) The rapport you have with parents and members of the community	1	2	3	0

Issues and Trends Questions

34. What do you think is the ideal grade organizational structure for a middle level school?
    - (1) 7-8-9
    - (2) 6-7-8
    - (3) 5-6-7
    - (4) 5-6-7-8
    - (5) 6-7-8-9
    - (6) 5-6
    - (7) 6-7
    - (8) 7-8
    - (9) 8-9
    - (10) Other:_____

35. Ability grouping is the assignment of students to classes based upon academic ability. Which statement best describes your opinion about academic ability grouping of students (excluding special education classes).
    - (1) There should be *no form* of ability grouping.
    - (2) Ability grouping of students *into certain classes* is appropriate.
    - (3) Ability grouping of students into any class is not appropriate, but grouping of students for instruction *within a class* is appropriate.

36. Identify any grade levels at which you feel greater emphasis should be placed upon intramural rather than interscholastic activities.
    - (1) All middle level grades
    - (2) Grades 8 and below
    - (3) Grades 7 and below
    - (4) Grades 6 and below
    - (5) Grade 5

37. In recent years technological advancements (e.g., satellite communication, instructional television, computer assisted instruction) have provided schools with opportunities for instructional methods not even thought of 10 to 20 years ago. Do you believe educational technology *has improved* the quality of the learning experiences for students in your school?
    - (1) Yes
    - (2) No

38. Do you believe educational technology *will improve* the quality of educational instruction for future students in your school?
    - (1) Yes
    - (2) No

39. Using the following scale, please indicate the degree to which you believe the middle level characteristics listed below are important to an instructionally effective middle level school.
    - (1) Little or no importance—absence of this characteristic will not affect the operation of the school.
    - (2) Somewhat important—presence of this characteristic adds to the quality of the school.
    - (3) Very important—presence of this characteristic is critical to a quality school.

CHARACTERISTIC	Little or No Importance	Somewhat Important	Very Important
(1) Interdisciplinary teams of 2-5 teachers sharing common students, common planning time, and housed in close proximity.	1	2	3
(2) Exploratory course offerings which provide required (not elective) curricular opportunities for all students, e.g., computers, family living, industrial technology, music.	1	2	3
(3) Adviser-advisee program regularly scheduled for 15 minutes or more during each classroom day.	1	2	3
(4) Cocurricular program separate from regular graded courses, but occurring during the school day, designed to provide students with the opportunity to pursue leadership roles, special interests, and socialization.	1	2	3
(5) Intramural activities offered for all students during or immediately after the regular classroom day.	1	2	3

40. Listed below are several factors which could be considered "roadblocks" preventing school leaders from doing the job they would like to do. Indicate the degree to which each factor has or has not been a roadblock to you over the past two years.

FACTOR	Not a Factor	Somewhat of a Factor	Serious Factor
(1) Collective bargaining agreement	1	2	3
(2) Deficient communication among administrative levels	1	2	3
(3) Inability to obtain funding	1	2	3
(4) Inability to provide teacher time for planning or professional development	1	2	3
(5) Insufficient space and physical facilities	1	2	3
(6) Lack of competent administrative assistance	1	2	3
(7) Lack of competent office help	1	2	3
(8) Lack of data about student skills and styles	1	2	3
(9) Lack of data on program successes/failures	1	2	3
(10) Lack of district-wide flexibility (all schools conform to same policy)	1	2	3
(11) Lack of knowledge among staff regarding programs for middle level students	1	2	3
(12) Lack of time for myself	1	2	3
(13) Long-standing tradition in the school/district	1	2	3
(14) Parents apathetic or irresponsible about their children	1	2	3
(15) Pressure from community	1	2	3
(16) Problem students (apathetic, hostile, etc.)	1	2	3
(17) Regulations or mandates from state or district governing boards	1	2	3
(18) Resistance to change by staff	1	2	3
(19) Superintendent or central office staff	1	2	3
(20) Teacher tenure	1	2	3
(21) Teacher turnover	1	2	3
(22) Time required to administer, supervise extracurricular activities	1	2	3
(23) Time taken by administrative detail at expense of more important matters	1	2	3
(24) Too large a student body	1	2	3
(25) Too small a student body	1	2	3
(26) Variations in the ability and dedication of staff	1	2	3

41. In which type of professional organization do you hold local, state, or national membership?
   (1) Professional teacher association or union; e.g.; NEA, AFT
   (2) Professional administrator association or union; e.g.; NASSP, NAESP
   (3) Subject area professional association; e.g.; National Council of Teachers of English
   (4) Honorary professional association; e.g.; Phi Delta Kappa
   (5) General professional association for the middle level; e.g.; National Middle School Association
   (6) Other:_____
   (7) I do not hold membership in a professional association.

42. Circle all of the following that apply to your district's support for your participation in the activities of professional educational organizations.
   (1) Discourages active participation in professional organizations
   (2) Encourages active participation in professional organizations
   (3) Pays my membership dues
   (4) Allows released time to attend meetings/conferences
   (5) Pays a portion (half or less) of my expenses to attend meetings/conferences
   (6) Pays all or most of my expenses to attend meetings/conferences

43. Circle the types of professional development activity in which you have been involved during the past two years.
    (1) National professional organization institute or conference (voluntary participation)
    (2) State professional organization activity (voluntary participation)
    (3) Activity conducted by private consultants at an out-of-district location (voluntary participation)
    (4) District activity required as part of employment
    (5) Other district activities (voluntary participation)
    (6) Enrollment in graduate courses at a college or university
    (7) State department or regional educational agency activity (voluntary participation)
    (8) State department or regional educational agency activity (required participation)
    (9) Principal center or academy (voluntary participation)
    (10) Other, specify:_____

44. Please identify the *three* most important skills/characteristics of an "excellent" middle level teacher. *Circle only three.*
    (1) Competence in subject matter knowledge
    (2) Competence in the use of varied methods of instruction
    (3) Competence in adjusting instruction to the varying learning styles and learning skills of the students
    (4) Competence in developing a positive relationship with students in the classroom
    (5) Competence in counseling students
    (6) Competence in working as a team member
    (7) Competence in using positive methods for student discipline
    (8) Competence in promoting positive student self-concept
    (9) Competence in employee behaviors and work habits (dependability, punctuality, attendance).
    (10) Competence in working with parents
    (11) Competence in working with colleagues

45. Much has been written about the tasks of American schools. Please rank the 11 statements below according to *your belief* about their relative importance as educational purposes.

    Assign a rank of "1" to the statement you consider most important, a rank of "2" to the next most important, until you assign a rank of "11" to the statement you consider least important.
    ____ (1) Acquisition of basic skills (reading, writing, speaking, computing, etc.)
    ____ (2) Appreciation for and experience with the fine arts
    ____ (3) Career planning and training in beginning occupational skills
    ____ (4) Development of moral and spiritual values
    ____ (5) Development of positive self-concept and good human relations
    ____ (6) Development of skills and practice in critical intellectual inquiry and problem solving
    ____ (7) Development of the skills to operate a technological society (engineering, scientific, etc.)
    ____ (8) Knowledge about and skills in preparation for family life (sex education, home management, problems of aging, etc.)
    ____ (9) Preparation for a changing world
    ____ (10) Physical fitness and useful leisure time sports
    ____ (11) Understanding of the American value system (its political, economic, social values, etc.)

Thank you for taking the time to complete this survey!
Please return the survey in the envelope provided.